Christ is My Beloved

A Devotional Study of Portraits of Christ in the Song of Solomon

George E Stevens

"My beloved is like a roe or young hart" (Song 2:9)

Scripture Truth Publications

First published 2009
Typeset and transferred to Digital Printing 2009
ISBN: 978-0-901860-84-2 (paperback)
Copyright © 2009 George E Stevens and Scripture Truth Publications
Illustrations copyright © 2009 George E Stevens

In scripture quotations from the Authorized Version, square brackets, [...], indicate
words which are not in the original language, but which were added to facilitate the
meaning in English.

Cover photograph ©iStockphoto.com/pushlama

Published by Scripture Truth Publications
31-33 Glover Street,
Crewe, Cheshire, CW1 3LD
Scripture Truth is an imprint of Central Bible Hammond Trust, a charitable trust
Typesetting by John Rice
Printed and bound by Lightning Source

CONTENTS

LIST OF HYMNS, MAPS, DIAGRAMS AND TABLES

Other hymns quoted may be found in "Psalms
and Hymns and Spiritual Songs: Selected 1978"
from Scripture Truth Publications.

Acknowledgements

On a broad basis, it is essential to thank servants of the Lord whom I have heard speaking on the Song of Songs intermittently over the last thirty years. More specific thanks go to the authors of the books listed in the bibliography at the back of this meditation from whom I gleaned many sweet meditations of Christ. The illustration of the Millennial Temple (used with permission) was based on the diagram found in *The Bible Knowledge Commentary: Old Testament* (Victor Books, 1985), page 1303. I especially wish to thank Dr Gordon Hughes and John Broadley for volunteering to read through the manuscript with a view to correcting my grammar and making suggestions as to parts that might be omitted or enhanced in some way.

Preface

The study of Christ in all the Scriptures is the most heart-warming occupation for any Christian. It corrects those who are going the wrong way in unbelief such as those on the Emmaus Road (Luke 24). It thrills the heart of young believers as they consider the amazing reliability of the Scriptures (as was my own experience when searching for Him in the subject of the Tabernacle in my formative years as a Christian). Furthermore, it always challenges the lives of those more mature in the faith in order that they may be moulded by the Holy Spirit into His likeness.

The Song of Solomon draws several portraits of our Lord Jesus as the object of one's love. This makes it one of the most exciting books of the Old Testament. It is a "song of loves" just like Psalm 45. As love is its base, then its study is not easily exhausted and its meditations help us to understand the Person and feelings of Christ much better. It is no small wonder that it is described as "The Song of Songs" (1:1).

On the other hand, it is not easy to interpret, as shown by the variety of meanings expressed in the commentaries that exist. I was personally troubled about this because the Lord is not the author of confusion. Therefore, in this book, I have sought, wherever possible, to use parallel scriptures to interpret the passages.

One of the major problems was to identify the Shulamite (the feminine of 'Solomon'), as there did not seem to be any specific biblical or historical character that fitted her description or the events relating to her and Solomon. I came to the conclusion that she is not an individual person, but rather Zion (the faithful remnant of Israel) herself. It was there that the Lord placed His name. Therefore, when King Solomon was crowned, he became "married" to his people.

I hope, therefore, that this book will encourage Christians to seek Christ in all the Scriptures in order that they may become more like Him. I also hope that it will encourage the children of Israel to recognise their Messiah and to know of a certainty that Israel will one day be spiritually re-born (as a nation) and once again serve the living and true God.

George E. Stevens

Introduction

The purposes in writing this book are to:

- reveal the appreciation of love between divine Persons and Zion;
- glorify the name of our Lord Jesus Christ;
- stir up the affections of the Christian reader for Him;
- promote Christ-like features and behaviour in believers; and
- show how the God-breathed scriptures are able to interpret themselves.

The Book of Kings tells us that Solomon wrote 1005 songs. This one is valued as the most excellent of them – the Song of Songs – **love** unsearchable, unquenchable, unfathomable and unpurchaseable being its subject (8:6-7). The Song seems to be related closely to Psalm 45 that is entitled 'A Song of Loves'.

The name 'Solomon' is related to the Hebrew *shalom* meaning 'peace'. It is a peace that results from being in harmony with God and our fellow men. Solomon was also given a second name – 'Jedidiah' which means 'Beloved of Yahweh' (2 Samuel 12:24-25). He is the

Beloved listed in the Song but, as we shall see, is typical of the Messiah, the Prince of Peace.

In Gibeon the LORD appeared to Solomon in a dream by night; and God said, *"Ask what I shall give thee."* And Solomon said, *"...And now, O LORD my God, thou hast made thy servant king instead of David my father: and I [am but] a little child: I know not how to go out or come in. And thy servant [is] in the midst of thy people which thou hast chosen, a great people, that cannot be numbered nor counted for multitude. Give therefore thy servant an understanding heart to judge thy people, that I may discern between good and bad: for who is able to judge this thy so great a people?"*

Solomon's answer pleased the Lord and He told Solomon, *"...Behold, I have done according to thy words: lo, I have given thee a wise and an understanding heart; so that there was none like thee before thee, neither after thee shall any arise like unto thee. And I have also given thee that which thou hast not asked, both riches, and honour: so that there shall not be any among the kings like unto thee all thy days. And if thou wilt walk in my ways, to keep my statutes and my commandments, as thy father David did walk, then I will lengthen thy days"* (1 Kings 3:5-9, 12-14).

It is the remembrance of this intimate revelation from the LORD that Solomon brings into this song.

Many commentators consider the Song of Solomon to have been written early in the life of Solomon because he declined spiritually as the years passed. Apparently, towards the end of his life, He returned to a close fellowship with God.

There are several interpretations of the Song. They include:

10

1. The more literal, that of a love story of a man and a woman. The courtship and wedding are described according to Middle Eastern custom.

2. The religious Jew's view that the Song pictures God's love for Israel His wife. In contrast to the purity, joy and vitality of the early love of Solomon and Shulamite, the book of Hosea gives us the striking contrast of latter-day Israel as the unfaithful and adulterous wife of Yahweh. God in His grace will yet restore her by grace.

3. Many Christian commentators interpret the Song of Songs as a picture of the Church as the Bride of Christ. God loves His only Son so much He has called out and prepared for Him a beautiful, virgin bride. This is illustrated in Genesis 24. Abraham's servant (type of the Holy Spirit) was sent by Abraham (type of the Father), into the far country to secure Rebekah as wife for his beloved son, Isaac, (type of Christ).

   This view is also indicated in the way that Paul speaks of the Corinthian assembly – an assembly that would represent the whole church: *"For I am jealous over you with godly jealousy: for I have espoused you to one husband, that I may present [you] as a chaste virgin to Christ. But I fear, lest by an means, as the serpent beguiled Eve through his subtilty, so your minds should be corrupted from the simplicity that is in Christ Jesus"* (2 Corinthians 11:2-3).

4. Some believe that the King is a picture of Christ our Lord and the Shulamite maiden pictures an individual believer who is seeking a closer, more intimate relationship with Jesus. Romans 7:1-4

contains an illustration where the woman depicts an individual believer who is married to Christ.

Although the above interpretations may be applied to the Song, it is my own opinion that the bride depicted in the Song specifically represents Zion (2 Kings 19:21; Isaiah 37:22) *the faithful remnant* of Israel in a future day. For that is where the Lord places His name. The bride and bridegroom in the Song share the same name – 'Shulamite'. In Hebrew, this is the feminine for 'Solomon'. Following the creation of the man and woman in the early chapters of Genesis, we find that God called *their* name Adam (Genesis 5:2). This is reflected later when the righteous Branch, the King whom God raises up to rule Judah and Israel, is called 'Yahweh our Righteousness' (Jeremiah 23:6) and His bride, Jerusalem, is called by the same name (Jeremiah 33:16). This King is the expected Messiah – the Christ. However, it is worthy of note that we have the terms 'the king' (1:12; 7:5) and 'King Solomon' (3:9, 11) in the Song. A similar occurrence comes in Psalm 72 where we read: *"Give the king thy judgements, O God, and thy righteousness unto the king's son."* The psalm then goes on to speak of the future kingdom under the reign of the king's son. It seems, therefore, that 'the king' (David) may well be representative of God Himself in the Song. Therefore, we see how precious the king's son (the Messiah) will be to both God and to Zion in a day to come.

God's past attitude of love and His promises towards Israel both add further support to this interpretation. In Deuteronomy 7:6-8 we read: *"For thou [art] an holy people unto the LORD thy God: the LORD thy God hath chosen thee to be a special people unto himself, above all people that [are] upon the face of the earth. The LORD did not set his love upon you, nor choose you, because ye [were] more in number than any people; for ye were the fewest of all people: but because* **the LORD** **loved you,** *and because he would keep the oath which he had sworn unto your fathers, hath the LORD brought you out with a mighty hand, and redeemed you out of the house of bondmen, from the hand of Pharaoh king of Egypt."*

Despite the fact that no musical accompaniment is indicated for this Song (as often seen in psalm titles) it, nevertheless, seems to be a kind of oratorio (musical drama) with the characters simply singing their parts rather than acting them. I suggest the principal characters in the Song include: King Solomon (the anointed), the Shulamite (a keeper of vineyards), the Daughters of Jerusalem (ladies of the royal court); the companions of Solomon; and, possibly, the brothers of the bride. Members of the bride's family may also speak.

There are a number of words that act as keys to unlock the Song. First, the one used to address the Beloved is *dod.* Second, the word used for the girlfriend and translated 'love' is *rayah.* However, there is another word used for 'love' itself in a number of verses (2:4, 5 and 7; 3:5 & 10; 5:8; 7:6; and 8:6-7). This is *ahabah.* Finally, the word used for 'spouse' is *kallah* referring to the girlfriend. One other hint in the identification of speakers is the fact that the bride uses the pronoun "me" regularly while the daughters use "we". However, we need to point out that it is very difficult to identify the speakers in all cases. In such situations, then, possibly, the voices are shared.

Chapter One
A Bundle of Myrrh

"A bundle of myrrh [is] my wellbeloved unto me; he shall lie all night betwixt my breasts." (Song 1:13)

Here there are three main parts which need to be explained:

1. the title the friend gives him – *my wellbeloved*;
2. the description of him – *a bundle of myrrh*;
3. the time – *dwell all night*; and,
4. the place she gives him – *betwixt my breasts*.

1. MY WELLBELOVED

The Hebrew word translated 'wellbeloved' is pronounced *dode* which comes from a root word meaning to 'boil'. Figuratively, it means 'to love'. Specifically, it means 'uncle'. Therefore, in this context, it speaks of the loved one – the object of this woman's heart.

The word is used in Isaiah 5:1, 7: *"Now will I sing to my wellbeloved a song of my **beloved** touching his vineyard. My* *wellbeloved has a vineyard in a very fruitful hill: ... for the vineyard of the* **LORD** *of hosts [is] the house of Israel, and the men of Judah his pleasant plant."*

We immediately discover that Yahweh is the wellbeloved of this song in Isaiah; while the vineyard represents the house of Israel. Both of these representations carry over into the Song of Solomon. However, there is a further implication given in this verse when we ask the question, "Who is speaking?" It could be Isaiah himself, or Yahweh speaking through the prophet. If the latter, then we have Yahweh speaking to Yahweh of hosts who is the owner of the vineyard. We are reminded of a similar occurrence in Psalm 110:1, 4 where David writes: *'The LORD said unto my Lord, Sit thou at my right hand, until I make thine enemies thy footstool. ... Thou [art] a priest for ever after the order of Melchizedek.'*

This relates to Yahweh (LORD) and *Adon* (Lord), the latter being the Lord Jesus Christ, the Son of God, who is called of God an high priest after the order of Melchizedek (Hebrews chapters 5–7). Therefore, it should follow that Yahweh of Hosts is also the Son of God. This seems to be verified by Psalm 24 that predicts the entry of Christ as the King of glory entering into Jerusalem. Verse 10 states: *"Who is this King of glory? The LORD of hosts, he [is] the King of glory. Selah."*

This is verified if we compare Isaiah 6 and John 12. The king seen in his glory is the Lord Jesus. He is called *"the King, the LORD of hosts"* (Isaiah 6:5), and John wrote of Him in these terms, *"These things said Esaias, when he saw his glory, and spake of him"* (John 12:41). Verse 1 of Isaiah 5 indicates that there is more than one Person in the Godhead. We can therefore see both the Eternal King and His Prince. We know from Colossians 1 that Christ is the

Son of the Father's love in whom the fullness dwells. In Colossians 2 He is the Christ in whom the fullness of the Godhead dwells bodily.

It is clear that the Son of God was ever the delight of His God and Father. Christ relates to those eternal scenes in Colossians 1 where the Creator is called the Son of the Father's love. Jesus verifies that He had the glory of such a position with the Father before the foundation of the world. *"I have glorified thee on the earth: I have finished the work which thou gavest me to do. And now, O Father, glorify thou me with thine own self with the glory which I had with thee before the world was"* (John 17:4-5). It is this glory which He has in His manhood today in heaven. He is ever the only-begotten Son who is in the bosom of the Father. Jesus could say, *"The Father loveth the Son, and sheweth him all things that himself doeth: and he will shew him greater works than these, that ye may marvel"* (John 5:20). And, *"Father, I will that they also, whom thou hast given me, be with me where I am; that they may behold my glory, which thou hast given me: for thou lovest me before the foundation of the world"* (John 17:24).

This love was also expressed while the Son of God was found in Manhood here on earth. At His baptism, God declared: *"This is my beloved Son, in whom I am well pleased"* (Matthew 3:17).

In His service, Jesus fulfilled the prophecy of Isaiah which also expresses the love of God: *"Behold, my servant, whom I have chosen; my beloved, in whom my soul is well pleased; I will put my spirit upon him, and he shall show judgement to the Gentiles. He shall not strive, nor cry;*

17

neither shall any man hear his voice in the streets. A bruised reed shall he not break, and smoking flax shall he not quench, till he send forth judgement unto victory" (Matthew 12:18-20; Isaiah 42:1).

He received honour and glory from God the Father when He was transfigured before three of His disciples: *"While he yet spake, behold, a bright cloud overshadowed them: and, behold, a voice out of the cloud, which said, This is my beloved Son, in whom I am well pleased; hear ye him"* (Matthew 17:5). Moses and Elijah were also with Him on that mountain representing the Law and the Prophets. God shows that His Son supersedes both by saying, *"Hear ye Him."*

The apostle Peter confirms this: *"For he received from God the Father honour and glory, when there came such a voice to him from the excellent glory, This is my beloved Son, in whom I am well pleased"* (2 Peter 1:17). All the delight of God rested in the Son. God could love Him complacently because He was worthy.

Furthermore, Christ could say in relation to His devotion even to the death of the cross: *"Therefore doth my Father love me, because I lay down my life that I might take it again"* (John 10:17). The Father can now love His Son compassionately as well as complacently.

Finally, He is declared to be the unique object of love in the purposes and will of God: *"To the praise of the glory of his grace, wherein he hath made us accepted in the beloved"* (Ephesians 1:6). Now we are loved with the same measure that the Father loves the Son (John 17:23, 26). The hymn writer puts it this way:

> *Loved with love that knows no measure,*
> *Save the Father's love to Thee;*

Blessed Lord, our hearts would treasure
All the Father's thoughts of thee.

(Miss C. A. Wellesley)

It is this unique Person that the girlfriend calls "My Beloved". There is no thought of sharing Him with anyone else. She possesses Him completely with the use of the word 'my'. We might well be reminded of the love of Mary Magdalene for the Lord Jesus. Finding His body gone from the tomb, she lingers there weeping. Not even the reassuring words of angels comfort her. Then Jesus Himself appears to her. Not recognising Him through her tears, she said: *"Sir, if thou have borne him hence, tell me where thou hast laid him, and I will take him away"* (John 20:15). There was only One who filled her heart. Only One for whom her love was so great. Only One she desired – her Jesus!

Yet it is written of the church of Ephesus, to whom Paul had revealed the Beloved (Ephesians 1:6), that they had lost their first love (Revelation 2:4). Christ was no longer the Beloved to their souls. Oh, that our eyes may be ever upon Him in order that our hearts continue in love as we run the marathon of faith! We should ever be: *"Looking unto Jesus the author and finisher of [our] faith; who for the joy that was set before him endured the cross, despising the shame, and is set down at the right hand of the throne of God. For consider him that endured such contradiction of sinners against himself, lest ye be wearied and faint in your minds"* (Hebrews 12:2-3).

How privileged the apostles were. John could write: *"That which was from the beginning, which we have heard, which we have seen with our eyes, which we have looked upon, and our hands have handled, of the Word of life; (for the life was manifested, and we have seen [it], and bear witness, and show unto you that eternal life, which was with the Father, and was manifested unto us;) that which we have seen and heard declare we unto you, that ye also may have fellowship with us: and truly our fellowship [is] with the Father, and with his Son Jesus Christ"* (1 John 1:1-3).

The apostles have indeed shared the Person of God's Son with us. Now we are able to apply to ourselves those words from the pen of Peter: *"Whom having not seen, ye love; in whom, though now ye see [him] not, yet believing, ye rejoice with joy unspeakable and full of glory ..."* (1 Peter 1:8).

He is our Beloved! We hear Him speaking to Peter, *"Simon, son of Jonas, lovest thou me more than these?"* Peter could not reply with a love having the force of the word which the Lord used. He, who had learned the lesson of humility from his previous denial of the Lord, could only say, *"Yea, Lord; thou knowest that I love* (have affection for) *thee."* However, it is that same Peter who wrote those words above in which he uses that same word for love that Jesus did, *"Whom having not seen, ye love."* So Peter is able to say along with each of us, **'He is *my* Beloved!'**

Another interesting point about the word 'beloved' is that it is the meaning of the name of David, which is written with the same Hebrew letters. In Jeremiah 30:9 we read that in the millennial day, *"... They shall serve the LORD their God, and **David their king**, whom I shall raise up unto them."* A united Israel and Judah will have one king.

It seems that Christ is given the name of David to show that He will be the Beloved in that day.

In Ezekiel 34:23-24, we find the same idea: *"And I will set up **one shepherd** over them, and he shall feed them, [even] my servant David; he shall feed them, and he shall be their shepherd. And I the LORD will be their God, and my servant **David a prince** among them; I the LORD have spoken it."*

A further confirmation of this is found in Hosea 3:5: *"Afterward shall the children of Israel return, and seek the LORD their God, and **David their king**; and shall fear the LORD and his goodness in the latter days."*

Some people have considered this David to be the resurrected David from the Old Testament times; but as one of the faithful of that time, he will be one of the friends of the Bridegroom. My personal opinion is that his portion will be a heavenly one. Where the term 'My servant David' is used in Ezekiel and Hosea, it seems to indicate that Christ is the overall Ruler who will be based in the heavenly Jerusalem (Revelation 21:22-27); while the term 'Prince' used by itself shows that there will be a vice-regent who has a similar office, but will rule on the planet's surface. This person would be of the tribe of Judah and would need to offer a sacrifice for his own sins as well as the people's.

Now the David of old was a type of the Lord Jesus as a warrior king. He was a man after God's own heart. A man whom God could like as well as love. But the name given to Solomon, namely, Jedidiah, also means the 'beloved of the Lord'. By contrast, his reign was one of peace and glory. Both types are seen in Christ, the King of kings and Lord of lords.

The character of the reign of Christ, the greater than Solomon, is predicted in Psalm 72. It is a reign of:

- righteousness (1-4);
- peace (7);
- power (8-11);
- mercy (12-14);
- prosperity (16); and,
- blessing (17).

We shall examine this reign in more detail later in the book.

It is written of Him in that day to come "*... His name shall be called Wonderful, Counsellor, The mighty God, The everlasting Father, The Prince of Peace. Of the increase of [his] government and peace [there shall be] no end, upon **the throne of David**, and upon his kingdom, to order it, and to establish it with judgement and with justice from henceforth even for ever. The zeal of the LORD of hosts will perform this*" (Isaiah 9:6-7).

2. A BUNDLE OF MYRRH

The Hebrew word for 'myrrh' is pronounced *mor*. Myrrh is known for its fragrant perfume and its bitter taste. In general, it reminds us that the fragrant blessings of God come to us as a result of the bitter sufferings of Christ.

The specific scriptural uses of myrrh are outlined as follows:

- Exodus 30:23 – part of the holy anointing oil used to *sanctify* the tabernacle and the priests;
- Esther 2:12 – part of Esther's treatment for *purification*;
- Psalm 45:8 – part of the oil of gladness that permeates the garments of the *king*;
- Proverbs 7:17 – part of the *perfuming* of a bed in preparation for physical love;
- Matthew 2:11 – one of the *gifts* presented to the Christ-child; and,
- John 19:39 – one of the *principal* spices used in *embalming* the body of Jesus for burial.

A. MYRRH IN THE HOLY ANOINTING OIL

The purpose of the holy anointing oil was to **sanctify** objects or people in the priestly service of the LORD. To 'sanctify' means to 'set apart' to God for His purpose and pleasure. This is relevant to the Lord Jesus who said: *"Say ye of him whom the Father hath sanctified, and sent into the world, Thou blasphemest; because I said, I am the Son of God"* (John 10:36). Furthermore, He said, *"And for their sakes I sanctify myself, that they also might be sanctified through the truth"* (John 17:19).

This oil was made up of: 500 shekels of pure myrrh; 250 sweet cinnamon; 250 sweet calamus; 500 cassia; and, a hin of oil olive. Olive oil speaks of the Holy Spirit of God. In Zechariah 4:6 we find a reference to the Spirit of the Lord in relation to two anointed ones who were represented by two olive trees. *"Not by might, nor by power, but*

by my spirit, saith the LORD of hosts." The Lord Jesus was not only anointed with the Spirit at His baptism; but He had also been conceived by the Holy Spirit. He was indeed the 'holy thing' – the Son of God! This is seen in the meal offering where oil is mingled with the flour (His conception by the Spirit) and used to anoint the bread (the Spirit coming upon Him at His baptism).

The word 'pure' has the sense of 'liberty'. The anointed Christ proclaimed liberty to the captives (Isaiah 61:1). The effect of the Spirit of the LORD anointing him is seen in the list of works in the accompanying verses. The characteristics of the Spirit, who indwelt Him, are found in Isaiah 11:2: *"And the spirit of the LORD shall rest upon him, the spirit of wisdom and understanding, the spirit of counsel and might, the spirit of knowledge and the fear of the LORD."*

These four sections may parallel the ingredients of the holy anointing oil. (As olive oil was the last in the list of the anointing oil, and the Spirit of the Lord is first in Isaiah 11, then the order of the latter should be reversed to get the parallel meaning). Olive oil speaking of the Spirit of the LORD; cassia (500) speaking of the spirit of wisdom and understanding; calamus (250) and cinnamon (250) the spirit of counsel and might; and, pure myrrh (500) *the spirit of knowledge and the fear of the LORD.* All are found in perfection in Christ.

At the same time, we must realise that it was Aaron and his sons who were anointed for priestly service in the book of Exodus. This is typical of Christ being our great high priest and of us being priests before God. (This was the intention of God for all Israel prior to the Aaronic priesthood). Christ appears in the presence of God for us. It is He who supports, sympathises and succours those who belong to Him. It is He who leads out our praises to God

the Father. It is He who once offered Himself by the eternal Spirit without spot unto God. He is the minister of good things to come. He is the One who is set on the right hand of the Majesty on high. He is the Mediator of a better covenant. He lives after the power of an endless life. We should try as much as possible to be as much like Him in our priestly role.

As Christians, today, we are privileged to be indwelt by the Holy Spirit of God (John 14:17; Ephesians 1:13). We should live lives which reveal His fruit (Galatians 5:22-23). Furthermore, we have undergone an act of anointing from the Holy One, which enables us to discern truth and error (1 John 2:20, 27). In a future day, Israel will be anointed by this same Spirit (Ezekiel 16).

B. MYRRH IN THE BEAUTY TREATMENT

Esther needed to be purified before going in to the presence of the king. Christ was One who was, in Himself, so pure that He was always acceptable to the eternal king – God. As to myrrh being used to purify, we find that Christ did no sin (pure actions), knew no sin (pure thoughts) and had no sin in Him (pure in His being). There was no man like Him. He was the second man, the Lord from out of heaven (1 Corinthians 15:47).

25

C. MYRRH IN THE GARMENTS OF THE KING (PSALM 45:8)

The Psalm in which we find these garments compares favourably to the Song of Songs. It is entitled, "A Song of Loves". Song 1:2 literally reads, *"Let him kiss me with the kisses of his mouth, for better are thy loves than wine"* (YLT).

The verse mentioned in Psalm 45 shows that the king had been anointed with the oil of gladness which relates back to the holy anointing oil. *"... A sceptre of righteousness [is] the sceptre of thy kingdom. Thou hast loved righteousness, and hated iniquity; therefore God, [even] thy God, hath anointed thee with the oil of gladness above thy fellows"* (Hebrews 1:8-9). These words show Him to be preeminent in His offices.

The fragrant garments relate to Christ in two offices, namely, those of priest and king. It is recorded of Christ as the Branch (Zechariah 6:12-13): *"And speak unto him, saying, Thus speaketh the LORD of hosts, saying, Behold, the man whose name [is] The BRANCH; and he shall grow up out of his place, and he shall build the temple of the LORD: Even he shall build the temple of the LORD; and he shall bear the glory, and shall sit and rule upon his throne; and he shall be a priest upon his throne; and the counsel of peace shall be between them both."*

Here we have the LORD of hosts speaking of Christ. Previously, we saw that Christ was the LORD of hosts. Is this a contradiction? No. Again, it shows us that there is more than one Person in the Godhead who claims equal honours. *"Before Abraham was, I am"*, Christ could say (John 8:58). But here Christ is seen as the man who is a priest for ever after the order of Melchizedek. The latter means, "my king is righteous". Christ is the righteous One. He is also King of Salem (peace). Christ is the Prince of peace. It is written of Melchizedek of old that he was without father, without mother, without descent, having neither beginning of days, nor end of life, but made like unto the Son of God (Hebrews 7:3). This shows us that the Son of God existed eternally. He did not become the Son of God when He became man for in that condition He had a mother. He always has been, is and will be the Son through whom God speaks.

And the Son of God is God! *"Unto the Son, [God saith], Thy throne, **O God**, [is] for ever and ever..."* (Hebrews 1:8). He will reign over this world for one thousand years following His appearance as King of kings and Lord of lords. He will come with the sword to deliver His people (Revelation 19:11-16). Next, we see Him with the sickle judging the nations (Revelation 14:14-16; Joel 3:12-14). Finally, we see Him holding the sceptre speaking of the authority of sovereign rule (Psalm 45:6). In that day, He will sit upon the throne of His glory (Matthew 25:31). Jerusalem itself will be the metropolis of the Earth being called *'The throne of the LORD'* (Jeremiah 3:17). Communication between the heavenlies and the Earth will be perfect (John 1:51).

His personal character is identified in the words of David: *"He that ruleth over men [must be] just, ruling in the fear of God. And [he shall be] as the light of the morning, [when] the sun riseth, [even] a morning without clouds"* (2 Samuel 23:3-4). Further details concerning His Person will be described as we go through the study.

The character of His kingdom has been listed previously on page 22; but it is a rule marked by righteousness (Isaiah 32:1; Jeremiah 23:5), peace (Micah 4:3; 5:5), power (5:9), prosperity (4:4) and privilege (Revelation 21:12-14). Israel will have priority over the nations (Micah 4:2) and the priesthood of Israel will be honoured

CHRIST IS MY BELOVED

and result in praise (Isaiah 61:6; Zephaniah 3:20). At the end of that time, when all rebellion has been put down, Christ will hand the kingdom back to God the Father. Then the Son will subject Himself to the Father in order that God might be all in all (1 Corinthians 15:24-28).

D. Myrrh in the Preparation of a Bed of Love (Proverbs 7:17)

In this scripture we find that a prostitute has prepared her bed for lovemaking. The emphasis is upon its fragrance being conducive to physical love or what might be called "the offices of love" (see Song 1:2). Of course, sexual intercourse outside of marriage is to be condemned. However, the verse shows us that there is **consolation** (comfort) in marital love. In Ezekiel 16:8, we read of a time of love between the LORD and Jerusalem: *"Now when I passed by thee, and looked upon thee, behold thy time [was] the time of love* (loves)*; and I spread my skirt over thee, and covered thy nakedness: yea, I sware unto thee, and entered into a covenant with thee, saith the Lord GOD, and thou becamest mine."*

Here the LORD claims Jerusalem as His wife. Such a union will be found perfected in the future: *"And this [is] his name whereby **he** shall be called, the LORD OUR RIGHT-EOUSNESS (Yahweh Tsidkenu)"* (Jeremiah 23:6); and, *"And this [is the name] wherewith **she** shall be called, the LORD our righteousness (Yahweh Tsidkenu)"* (33:16).

However, as the history of Jerusalem shows, her desire for the LORD has not been constant for in Ezekiel 23:17 we read, *"And the Babylonians came to her into the bed of love* (loves)*, and they defiled her with their whoredom, and she was polluted with them, and her mind was alienated from them."*

Nevertheless, the promise of the LORD remains sure: *"And I will betroth thee unto me for ever; yea, I will betroth thee unto me in **righteousness**, and in **judgement**, and in **loving kindness**, and in **mercies**. I will even betroth thee unto me in **faithfulness**, and thou shalt know the LORD"* (Hosea 2:19-20).

Here we discover what the interpretation of the fragrance of the bed of love is. The loves of the king are for His earthly bride of Zion. Loves which, without doubt, may be applied to the heavenly bride (the church) also. It is wonderful to know that they also apply to each individual believer! What consolation! What comfort!

E. MYRRH AS A GIFT TO THE CHRIST-CHILD (MATTHEW 2:11)

"And when they were come into the house, they saw the young child with Mary his mother, and fell down, and worshipped him: and when they had opened their treasures, they presented unto him gifts; gold, and frankincense, and myrrh."

There seem to be three things to note here. Firstly, these

gifts were suitable for a king; secondly, they were very valuable; and, thirdly, they accompanied the worship of these men.

Generally, it is said that gold is so-called because of its shining. It therefore represents the glory of God. The Lord Jesus Christ is the brightness of God's glory (Hebrews 1) and the express image of His Person. This is further expressed in Revelation 21:23 which speaks of the glory of God lighting up the holy city and the Lamb being the lamp thereof. He is the Source of God's glory! He is God!

Frankincense is so-called because of its whiteness or, possibly, the whiteness of its smoke when burning. It represents purity and dependence. Thereby, it expresses the perfection of Christ which rises to God the Father as a sweet fragrance on the one hand, and His dependence upon God as a prayerful man (Revelation 8:4) on the other. This seems to be verified by its use in the meal offering of old (Leviticus 2). The whole offering speaking of the absolute perfection of Christ in His devotion to the will of God. There the frankincense was for the LORD. It follows that, *"No man knows the Son, but the Father."*

As previously mentioned, the myrrh is so-called from its bitterness. It represents the sufferings of Christ, and the sweet fragrance of blessing which emanated from them to both God and Man.

Myrrh was a gift fit for the King of the Jews because it was a principal spice. It reminds us of the King who will be King of kings and Lord of lords – the pre-eminent One! He is the chiefest among ten thousand. Colossians 1 outlines His glories and in verse 18 we see the reasons for them, *"That in all [things] he might have the pre-eminence."* He is the image of the invisible God, and the firstborn (first in rank) of every creature.

The substance is not only valued for its fragrance; but is said to have antiseptic qualities which help to heal wounds and diseases. This reminds us that Christ is the Great Physician. He had power over the deep, the devil, disease and death (Luke 8). Yet the Spirit of the Lord also sent Him to heal the broken-hearted and to preach recovery of sight to the blind.

These wise men were *Magi*, that is to say, a class of priests or astronomers from ancient Persia. They were clearly men of standing and wealth. Yet they bowed before the Christ-child whom they believed to be the King of the Jews. Doing so they offered the myrrh as one of their gifts. They were examples of good men bringing forth from the good treasure of their hearts that which was good in both the moral and practical senses. Christ is worthy of glory and honour. He is the One whom God has glorified and to whom every knee shall bow. *"Wherefore God hath highly exalted him, and given him a name which is above every name: that at the name of Jesus every knee should bow...and [that] every tongue should confess that Jesus Christ is Lord, to the glory of God the Father"* (Philippians 2:9-10).

F. MYRRH USED IN EMBALMING IN PREPARATION FOR BURIAL (JOHN 19:39)

Here we find the culmination of the sufferings of Christ. He has given Himself up to death. Nicodemus, a secret disciple comes forward publicly with the mixture of spices with which to bury His body. Joseph of Arimathæa, another secret disciple, had come out publicly to beg for the body of Jesus from Pilate and had given up his own tomb for the burial of Christ's body. Mary, the sister of Martha, had anointed the body of Jesus prematurely. *"Against the day of my burying hath she kept this"*, Jesus said.

So, simply, the myrrh is active as a preservative in the context of embalming. It reminds us that Christ is the Saviour. The One who is ready, willing, able and seeking to save from wrath and sins and every evil work and this present evil world and from death. *"He is able **to save them to the uttermost** that come unto God by him, seeing he ever lives to make intercession for them"* (Hebrews 7:25).

It also reminds us that He is both the Deliverer and Preserver of Israel. Romans 11:26 says, *"There shall come out of Sion* [Zion] **the Deliverer.***"* His description as Saviour is found in Isaiah 43:1-3: *"But now thus saith the LORD that created thee, O Jacob, and he that formed thee, O Israel, Fear not: for I have redeemed thee, I have called [thee] by my name; thou [art] mine. When thou passest through the waters, I [will be] with thee; and through the rivers, they shall not overflow thee: when thou walkest through the fire, thou shalt not be burned; neither shall the flame kindle upon thee. For I [am] the LORD thy God, the Holy One of Israel,* **thy Saviour.***"*

The opening verse of the book of Jude pinpoints Christ in the myrrh character: *"Jude, the servant of Jesus Christ, and brother of James, to them that are sanctified by God the father, and* **preserved in Jesus Christ,** *[and] called…"*

A bundle of myrrh is an allusion to the bags of perfumes and sweet powders which people carried in their bosoms in order to revive their spirits or, if a gift, to remember the giver. And, before leaving this section on myrrh, some consideration should be given to the term 'bundle'. According to Young's concordance the word means 'a thing compressed'. If we apply this to Christ, we see the sufferings borne in manhood. In the wilderness, He was tested by the devil. He overcame with the words, *'It is written…'* When found at the grave of Lazarus, He shed tears as He saw his loved ones mourning. He shed tears as He experienced the grief that the death of a loved one caused. He

shed tears as He contemplated the results of sin's effect upon this world. Yet we see God glorified in the command, *'Lazarus, come forth.'* The one who had died responded immediately.

We see Christ in the Garden of Gethsemane. The very name of the place suggests pressure by its meaning – 'the place of the oil press'. In the shadow of the cross, He sweat as it were great drops of blood. The agony of that moment was so immense. Yet He gained the victory and gave joy to the heart of God with the words, *"O my Father, if it be possible, let this cup pass from me: nevertheless, not as I will, but as thou [wilt]"* (Matthew 26:39).

This triumph constantly marked his life as a man here, for we read in Hebrews 5:7-9: *"Who in the days of his flesh, when he had offered up prayers and supplications with strong crying and tears unto him that was able to save him from death, and was heard in that he feared; though he were a Son, yet learned he obedience by the things which he suffered; and being made perfect, he became the author of eternal salvation unto all them that obey him."*

Men took Him by wicked hands! How they abused the Lord of life! Yet He accepted that suffering. He was led as a sheep to the slaughter. He who could say, *'I am [he]'* and cause His enemies to go backward and prostrate themselves to Him in enforced worship (John 18:6), suffered in silence for righteousness' sake.

We are reminded of the incense beaten small and burned in the holiest of all (Leviticus 16:12) which is a picture of the preciousness of Christ emanating from the way in which He behaved during times of suffering. That preciousness filling that holy place prior to the high priest entering with the blood of atonement. The hymnwriter puts it this way:

> *The veil is rent: our souls draw near*
> *Unto the throne of grace;*
> *The merits of the Lord appear,*
> *They fill the holy place.*

(J.G.Deck)

But the physical and mental torture pressed on Him by men was nothing compared to the suffering upon the cross where His holy soul was made an offering for sin. There He endured the judgement of God against sin! Well might the worship in the same writer's words rise from our hearts:

> *When we see Thee, as the Victim,*
> *Nailed to the accursed tree,*
> *For our guilt and folly stricken,*
> *All our judgement borne by Thee,*
> *Lord, we own with hearts adoring,*
> *Thou hast washed us in Thy blood:*
> *Glory, glory everlasting,*
> *Be to Thee, Thou Lamb of God!*

(J. G. Deck)

3. LIE ALL NIGHT

This term means 'To pass the night'. We read in Romans 13:11-12, *"And that, knowing the time, that now [it is] high time to awake out of sleep: for now [is] our salvation nearer than when we believed.* **The night is far spent**, *the day is at hand: let us therefore cast off the works of darkness, and let us put on the armour of light."*

'Night' therefore indicates the period of time when the Lord is absent. For Zion, it may indicate the time of the Great Tribulation (Isaiah 60:1-2) or Jacob's trouble. A time of great judgements and trial. Throughout it all, the fragrance of His Person refreshes and comforts her. However, when the day dawns then the Messiah will arise as the Sun of righteousness with healing in His wings (Malachi 4:2). This speaks of the day of His appearing as the King of kings. He will set up the everlasting kingdom, which will last for a millennium; but never be overthrown. Israel will be greatly blessed at that time. Zion will be the earthly bride of the Lord.

Until the day of His presence, she remembers Him by the bundle of myrrh that lies between her breasts. Christians, of this age, may bear Him as a bundle of myrrh between their breasts as they are called upon to remember the Lord Jesus Christ by partaking of the Lord's Supper. We read of its institution in Luke 22:19-20: "*And he took bread, and gave thanks, and brake [it], and gave unto them, saying, This is my body which is given for you: **this do in remembrance of me***. *Likewise also the cup after supper, saying, This cup [is] the New Testament in my blood, which is shed for you.*" The fragrance of His Person and work emanate from that remembrance.

The apostle Paul expands upon the thought of this remembrance in 1 Corinthians 11:23-30: "*For I have received of the Lord that which also I delivered unto you, that the Lord Jesus the [same] night in which he was betrayed took bread: and when he had given thanks, he brake [it], and said, Take, eat: this is my body, which is broken for you: this do in remembrance of me. After the same manner also [he took] the cup, when he had supped, saying, This cup is the new testament in my blood: this do ye, as oft as ye drink it, in remembrance of me. For as often as ye eat this bread, and*

35

drink this cup, ye do shew the Lord's death till he come. Wherefore whosoever shall eat this bread, and drink [this] cup of the Lord, unworthily, shall be guilty of the body and blood of the Lord. But let a man examine himself, and so let him eat of [that] bread, and drink of [that] cup. For he that eateth and drinketh unworthily, eateth and drinketh damnation to himself, not discerning the Lord's body. For this cause many [are] weak and sickly among you, and many sleep."

The passage may be divided by seven **looks**:

1. Look Up!	5. Look Out!
2. Look Back!	6. Look In!
3. Look To!	7. Look At!
4. Look On!	

1. LOOK UP!

This is found in the words, *"For I have received of the Lord that which also I delivered unto you…"*. The apostle stated that the source of this instruction came directly from the Lord Himself. This is revelation! Therefore, its authority cannot be denied. Paul then said that he had passed on this instruction to the Christians at Corinth. This is inspiration! It was now the responsibility of the Christians to obey God's word.

2. LOOK BACK!

This is found in the words, *"That the Lord Jesus the [same] night in which he was betrayed took bread: and when he had given thanks, he brake [it], and said, Take, eat: this is my body, which is broken for you: this do in remembrance of me. After the same manner also [he took] the cup, when he had supped, saying, This cup is the New Testament in my blood…"*.

A supper was the main meal of the day in Israel. It was eaten in the evening. However, this was also the Passover celebration that marked the deliverance of Israel from the bondage of Egypt so long ago. The Lord Jesus gives this supper a completely different character. The lamb that was slain was now to be recalled in the bread and the wine because the lamb of the Old Testament was a type of the Christ of the New. So the bread represented the body of Christ that was "for" the disciples and the wine represented the New Covenant established on the grounds of His shed blood.

(The New Covenant is the consummation of all other covenants combined. It is based on God's unmerited favour to mankind shown in the sacrifice of Christ. It is an everlasting covenant of blessing. Any other will never supersede it).

3. LOOK TO!

"This do ye, as oft as ye drink [it], in remembrance of me." The Lord, in these terms, commands Christians to do the same thing in remembrance of Him. So when believers partake of the Lord's Supper, it is specifically in order to remember Him. He may be recalled in hymn or song; in prayer and praise; or through the reading of God's word; but the actual act of remembrance is taking and eating the bread and taking and drinking the wine. If you believe in the Lord Jesus then you must love Him. If so you will want to keep His commandments. Look to this one and obey!

4. LOOK ON!

"For as often as ye eat this bread, and drink this cup, ye do shew the Lord's death till he come." Christians who partake of the Lord's Supper are to do so with the coming of Christ in mind. He will come again to receive all believers to Himself. They will be for ever with the Lord. This reminds us of the urgency there is attached to this remem-

brance of our Lord Jesus. If we are exercised about breaking bread, then let us not procrastinate because the coming of the Lord is near.

5. Look Out!

It is a solemn matter to remember the Lord in this way. The words, *"Wherefore whosoever shall eat this bread, and drink [this] cup of the Lord, unworthily, shall be guilty of the body and blood of the Lord. ... "* It is important to come to the Supper with the right attitude. The supper should not be eaten as an ordinary meal. The Corinthians themselves had a meal or love feast which they thought was the Lord's Supper, but it was marked by greed and even some drunkenness (1 Corinthians 11:20-22). May we be preserved from this.

6. Look In!

This look is expressed in the words, *"But let a man examine himself, and so let him eat of [that] bread, and drink of [that] cup. For he that eateth and drinketh unworthily, eateth and drinketh damnation to himself... "*. Any Christians intending to remember the Lord Jesus should be on their knees beforehand examining themselves. The word 'examine' relates to proving metals. It has the sense of purifying ourselves for the approval of God. So we would confess our sins knowing that He is faithful and just to forgive our sins and cleanse us from all unrighteousness. We should then be free to partake of the Supper.

7. Look At!

The words, *"...not discerning the Lord's body. For this cause many [are] weak and sickly among you, and many sleep"* show us that we must have a clear knowledge of what we are doing when we partake of the Lord's Supper. We need to know what the emblems of the bread and wine represent. If we don't then we may well be eating and drinking judgement to ourselves. Some believers at Corinth were weak and sickly and others falling asleep (dying) because they were negligent in the way that they took this supper. Let us take care how we approach the presence of the Lord on this occasion.

4. Betwixt my Breasts

This is a place of closest affection and intimacy. It is the place of the heart which speaks of love and life affecting the will. Her Beloved was both to her. He was her first love. Yet in Isaiah 66:11 we see that it is from the breasts of Jerusalem that there is satisfaction in her consolations and delight in the abundance of her glory. She would give these to her Beloved. Using words from a well-known hymn it could be said of her:

> *The bride eyes not her garment,*
> *But her dear bridegroom's face;*
> ***She*** *does not gaze at glory,*
> *But on **her** King of Grace;*
> *Not at the crown He giveth,*
> *But on His pierced hand;*
> *The Lamb is all the glory*
> *Of Immanuel's land.*
>
> *(Mrs. A. R. Cousin, based on S. Rutherford)*

Oh that we might do the same in order that our hearts be moved to adore and praise the altogether lovely One who loved us and gave Himself for us!

Chapter Two
A Cluster of Camphire

"My beloved [is] unto me [as] a cluster of camphire in the vineyards of Engedi." (Song 1:14)

In this chapter we will examine:

1. the scriptural meaning and uses of 'camphire';
2. what is meant by a 'cluster'; and,
3. why in the vineyards of Engedi.

1. CAMPHIRE

According to H.B. Tristram in his book entitled *The Natural History of the Bible*, camphire is apparently a shrub which grows to a height of almost three metres. It has dark bark, pale green foliage and clusters of white and yellow blossoms of strong fragrance. The latter are prized for their perfume, while the leaves of the plant are pounded into a powder and mixed with water to produce a paste of red dye. People who are able to afford it use the dye on the palms of their hands, the soles of their feet and their nails. Apparently, it is used to check perspiration. Interestingly, it has survived to this day in Engedi.

The Hebrew word for it is *kopher* that comes from a root word *kaphar* meaning 'to cover'. An interesting thought when people use the dye to cover parts of their body. Further meanings include: satisfaction, ransom, bribe, pitch and village.

In Exodus 30:12 the word is used to denote the half a shekel of **ransom** money given by each man as an offering to the LORD. The purpose was to make atonement for their souls.

Applying the key of Christ being the Anti-type of the beloved, we find that there are scriptures linking Him directly to the idea of a ransom. In 1 Timothy 2:5-6, we read: *"For [there is] one God, and one mediator between God and men, the man Christ Jesus; who gave himself a ransom for all, to be testified in due time."* Matthew 20:28 and Mark 10:45 say: *"… The Son of man came not to be ministered unto, but to minister, and to give his life a ransom for many."*

So Christ gave His life as a ransom for **all**; while, as the Son of man, He gave His life as a ransom for **many**. Is there a contradiction here? No! As the Mediator Christ gave His life as the corresponding price that would purchase the deliverance of all men. However, as not all men believe in Him and accept His sacrifice then the ransom only becomes effective (i.e. purchases) the 'many'.

2. A CLUSTER

The Hebrew word for 'cluster' is *eshkol*. In Genesis 40:10 we find: *"And in the vine [were] three branches: and it [was] as though it budded, [and] her blossoms shot forth; and the clusters thereof brought forth ripe grapes..."*

Numbers 13:24 speaks of the cluster that was taken from the brook of Esh-col which had to be carried upon a staff and by two men. Such fruit was evidence that the land of Canaan was flowing with milk and honey.

Isaiah 65:8 reads: *"Thus saith the LORD, as the new wine is found in the cluster, and [one] saith, Destroy it not; for a blessing [is] in it: so will I do for my servants' sakes, that I may not destroy them all."*

We have seen that the ransom money was given in Exodus 30 to be an offering to the LORD for an atonement for their souls. Yet the same LORD said, *"For the life of the flesh [is] in the blood: and I have given it to you upon the altar to make an atonement for your souls: for it [is] the blood [that] maketh an atonement for the soul"* (Leviticus 17:11). In the New Testament we do not find the word atonement; but we do find a cluster of truth linked with the sacrifice of Christ:

Redemption: to loose by a price (1 Peter 1:18-19); and, to acquire from a market (Revelation 5:9).

Reconciled: a complete change e.g. enemies become allies (Romans 5:10).

Forgiveness: to send away [sins] (Ephesians 1:7); and, to be gracious toward (Ephesians 4:32).

Justification: to clear of every charge – declare or make righteous (Romans 5:9).

Peace: concord or union (Colossians 1:20).

Cleansing: to make clean or clear (1 John 1:7).

Salvation: to make sound or safe (Ephesians 2:5).

Sanctification: to set apart to God for His purpose, possession and pleasure (Hebrews 13:12).

Access: a leading into (Ephesians 2:18; Hebrews 10:19).

Victory: to triumph over an enemy (1 Corinthians 15:57; Revelation 12:11).

Washed: to bathe or wash clean (Revelation 1:5; 7:14-15).

There can be no greater cluster of divine work than this. But in Micah 7:1-2 we read: *"Woe is me! for I am as when they have gathered the summer fruits, as the grape gleanings of the vintage: [there is] no cluster to eat: my soul desired the firstripe fruit. The good [man] is perished out of the earth: and [there is] none upright among men..."*

These verses give rise to a saying among the Jews: *"After the death of Jose Ben Joezer, a man of Tzereda, and Jose Ben Jochanan, a man of Jerusalem, the clusters ceased according to Micah 7:1."*[1] Furthermore, they say: *"What is* **Esh-col**, *a cluster? It is* **ish shehaccol bo***, a man that has all things in him."*[2]

These words can only **truly** relate to One, even the Lord Jesus Christ. Eight of the clusters of truth concerning Him are listed below.

1. He fulfilled the cluster of God's word. *"And he said unto them, These [are] the words which I spake unto you, while I was yet with you, that all things must be fulfilled, which were written in the law of Moses, and*

---

[1] Mimah Sotah 9.9, cited in John Gill *Exposition of the Book of Solomon's Song.*
[2] T. Bab. Temurah, folio 15.2, *op. cit.*

CHRIST IS MY BELOVED

[in] the prophets, and [in] the Psalms, concerning me"
(Luke 24:44).

2. As noted previously, the cluster relating to the Spirit
   abode in Him – the Spirit of the LORD rests upon
   Him: the spirit of wisdom and understanding, the
   spirit of counsel and might, the spirit of knowledge
   and of the fear of the LORD (Isaiah 11:2).

3. In the day of His appearing the cluster surrounding
   His name is revealed for He shall be called
   Wonderful, Counsellor, The mighty God, The
   everlasting Father, The Prince of Peace (Isaiah 9:6).

4. He is the Word who subsisted in the beginning;
   who was face to face with God; who was God; who
   always existed in this way; who made all things;
   and, the One in whom there is life (John 1:1-4).

5. Colossians 1 tells us that He is the Son of the
   Father's love; the Redeemer; the Image of the invisible God; the Firstborn of every creature; the
   Creator; the Sustainer of all; the Head of the
   church; the Beginning; the firstborn from the dead;
   and, hence, the Pre-eminent One.

6. In Hebrews 1 we find Him as the Son; the Heir of
   all; the Maker of the ages; the Brightness of God's
   glory; the Express Image of God's Person; the
   Upholder of all; the Purgator of sins; and, the
   Exalted One.

7. He is made unto us wisdom, righteousness and
   sanctification (1 Corinthians 1:30).

8. God was manifested in the flesh, justified in the
   Spirit, seen of angels, preached unto the Gentiles,
   believed on in the world, received up into glory
   (1 Timothy 3:16).

An unknown hymnwriter expressed the preciousness of Christ well when he wrote:

Father, how precious unto Thee
Is Thy beloved Son,
In whom Thou dost perfection see,
Thy holy, blessed One!

When He in flesh the desert passed,
He loved to do Thy will;
His food it was, through to the last,
Thy pleasure to fulfil.

Only-begotten, He revealed
Thyself unto Thy praise:
The Father, until then concealed,
Was seen in all His ways.

As in His life, so in His death,
He was devoted still;
For us in love resigned His breath,
Obedient to Thy will.

He glorified Thee on the earth:
Thy work by Him was done;
And Thou, who knewest all His worth,
Didst glorify Thy Son.

Now crowned and seated on Thy throne,
He is Thy joy and rest;
And we who are by grace Thine own
In Him are fully blest.

He, preciousness itself to Thee,
To us is precious too;
We every beauty in Him see,
And Thine own glory view.

(Anon.)

3. In the Vineyards of Engedi

A. Engedi

Engedi is a town on the Western shore of the Salt Sea, in the wilderness of Judah. The most common meaning of *Engedi* seems to be 'fountain of a kid'. Its original name was Hazazon-Tamar (pruning of the palm). Engedi was a place of safety for men (1 Samuel 23:29). Also it was a rocky area renowned for its wild goats (1 Samuel 24:1). In fact the Psalmist uses these creatures to emphasise the idea of safety when he writes, *'The high hills [are] a refuge for the wild goats...'* (Psalm 104:18). It is a place of future blessing (Ezekiel 47:10) in the Millennial Kingdom. It is written: *"And by the river upon the bank thereof, on this side and on that side, shall grow all trees for meat, whose leaf shall not fade, neither shall the fruit thereof be consumed: it shall bring forth new fruit according to his months, because their waters they issued out of the sanctuary: and the fruit thereof shall be for meat, and the leaf thereof for medicine"* (Ezekiel 47:12).

If we put together the thought of the sanctuary, safety, the river, the rocks and the wilderness contained in the place and meaning of Engedi, we may conclude: *"Behold, a king shall reign in righteousness, and princes shall rule in judgement. And a man shall be as an hiding place from the wind, and a covert from the tempest; as rivers of water in a dry place, as the shadow of a great rock in a weary land"* (Isaiah 32:1-2).

This Man was, in His rejection by men, identified as Jesus of Nazareth by the Gentile governor, Pontius Pilate: *"Behold the man!...Behold your King!"* (John 19:5, 14). In verse 19 of the same chapter we read that Pilate wrote a title, and put it on the cross. It said, "Jesus of Nazareth the King of the Jews." When challenged about this by the chief priests, he would not change the title in any way. He is our refuge! Thomas bowed to this man in His resurrected form and said, "My Lord, and my God." This man is none other than the Word become flesh. He is our refuge, and strength, a very present help in trouble as Psalm 46 indicates. The result is that we are not fearful.

The One who became a man in order to set up the Kingdom of God upon earth was also the One who had to die on account of our sinfulness. *"Ought not Christ to have suffered these things, and to enter into his glory?"* (Luke 24:26). God *"hath made him [to be] sin for us, who knew no sin; that we might be made the righteousness of God in him"* (2 Corinthians 5:21).

He is able to deliver us from every contrary wind of doctrine. He shelters us from the full rage of the storms of life. He supplies the water of life by the power of the Spirit. He provides the refreshing shade, which enables us to grow in grace and the knowledge of Himself. Like the rock, He is the same yesterday, and today, and for ever.

B. VINEYARD

The meaning of vineyard is 'an enclosed place'. The vineyards are protected from animals (like little foxes) and the wind by high walls or fences. Luke 13:32 shows us a man who was a grown-up fox, namely, Herod. He was a man of evil acts. The lust of the eye, lust of the flesh and the pride of life were apparent in him. These led to him executing John the Baptist. He and his men treated Christ shamefully. And, it was like-minded men by whose wicked hands our Saviour was crucified and slain.

The vineyard's fruit is used to manufacture wine, which *cheers God and man* (Judges 9:13, N.Tr.). But what exactly does this fruit typify? The answer lies in Isaiah 5:7. There the LORD looks for **judgement and righteousness** from His pleasant plant. These two things meet in the verse quoted above where the king shall reign in righteousness and the princes shall rule in judgement. Justice and judgement are the habitation of His throne. In the day of His reign, *"The moon shall be confounded, and the sun ashamed, when the LORD of hosts shall reign in Mount Zion, and in Jerusalem, and before his ancients gloriously"* (Isaiah 24:23). Along the same lines we read, *"In that day shall the branch of the LORD be beautiful and glorious…"* (Isaiah 4:2).

These are happy thoughts for the Christian because we know *"When Christ, [who is] our life shall appear, then shall we also appear with him in glory"* (Colossians 3:4). We may well say, "Come, Lord Jesus. Come!" In the meanwhile, we like this girlfriend should be gazing upon Him whom we love in all His glory in order that we might be changed into the same image.

> *Royal robes shall soon invest Thee,*
> *Royal splendours crown Thy brow;*
> *Christ of God, our souls confess Thee*
> *King and Sovereign even now;*

Thee we reverence,
Thee obey,
Own Thee Lord and Christ alway.

(R. Holden)

Chapter Three
The Apple Tree

"As the apple tree among the trees of the wood, so [is] my beloved among the sons." (Song 2:3)

In this verse we will examine the meanings of:

1. the trees of the wood;
2. the sons;
3. the apple tree; and, finally,
4. the comparison made.

1. THE TREES OF THE WOOD

The Hebrew word for 'tree' may be translated as 'tree', 'wood', 'timber' or 'stick'; while the word for 'wood' may also mean 'forest'. In Judges 9:7-16, young Jotham tells a prophetic parable relating to Abimelech (who had murdered his seventy brothers) and to the people of Shechem. In it, he compares men to certain types of tree and is suggesting that **a king** be found. The bramble, which was quite unsuitable to rule, represented Abimelech. The cedars of Lebanon represented **the men** of Shechem. Jotham said, *"If ye then have dealt truly and sincerely with Jerubbaal (Gideon) and with his house this day, [then] rejoice ye in Abimelech, and let him also rejoice in you: but if* *not, let fire come out from Abimelech, and devour the men of Shechem, and the house of Millo; and let fire come out from the men of Shechem, and from the house of Millo, and devour Abimelech"* (Judges 9:19-20). The fire was sparked off only three years later.

From this parable we are able to glean that trees may represent men and leaders of men. In Psalm 1:1-3 we find that the godly man is compared to a tree planted by the rivers of waters. Proverbs 11:30 tells us that the fruit of the righteous is a tree of life. While Psalm 92:12 indicates that the righteous grow as the cedar. Amos 2:9 informs us that the oak is renowned for its strength.

This is supported by Daniel 4 where Nebuchadnezzar is symbolized by a tree in his vision. *"It [is] thou, O king, that art grown and become strong: for thy greatness is grown, and reacheth unto heaven, and thy dominion to the end of the earth"* (Daniel 4:22). Furthermore, a whole chapter (Ezekiel 31) is taken up with a description of Pharaoh and all his multitude. Like the Assyrian, he was compared to a cedar of Lebanon. He was great, beautiful, strong, spreading and a refuge; but he was proud.

Isaiah 44:14 lists some of the trees of the forest as the cedar, cypress, oak and ash, while, in 41:19, the LORD groups together the cedar, shittah, myrtle and oil and, furthermore, the fir, pine and box trees. They are trees of **excellence** (Isaiah 60:13) being called "the glory of Lebanon". Furthermore, these trees are linked with the *blessing of the LORD* (Isaiah 55:13; 61:11). It suggests that the trees of the wood are men of nobility – leaders of the people who come under God's blessing and guidance.

2. THE SONS

In the comparison made in this verse, the trees of the wood represent the sons. If we link this to the "excellent" then we may see that these may well represent the other princes of the land, past and present. For example, we could look at the genealogy of Jesus Christ as found in Matthew 1:1-17 and find many kings of Judah from David onwards:

"And Jesse begat David the king; and David the king begat Solomon of her [that had been the wife] of Urias; and Solomon begat Roboam; and Roboam begat Abia; and Abia begat Asa; and Asa begat Josaphat; and Josaphat begat Joram; and Joram begat Ozias; and Ozias begat Joatham; and Joatham begat Achaz; and Achaz begat Ezekias; and Ezekias begat Manasses; and Manasses begat Amon; and Amon begat Josias; and Josias begat Jechonias and his brethren, about the time they were carried away to Babylon…" (verses 6-11).

We stop at Jechonias because it was written of him, *"Thus saith the LORD, Write ye this man childless, a man [that] shall not prosper in his days; for no man of his seed shall prosper, sitting upon the throne of David, and ruling any more in Judah"* (Jeremiah 22:30).

Although, legally the royal line of Judah continued to Joseph the husband of Mary and to Jesus Christ, the sons listed above are the ones exempt from the curse placed upon Jechonias. We can immediately see that for Christ to prosper as king in Judah, then He would have to be legally of David's line yet not of the seed of Jechonias. God achieved this through His conception by the Holy Spirit and the virgin birth.

3. THE APPLE TREE

The Hebrew word *tappuach* occurs three other times in this song: *"Comfort (or support) me with apples: for I [am] sick of love"* (2:5); *"The smell of thy nose like apples"* (7:8); and, *"I raised thee up under the apple tree"* (8:5). While, in

Proverbs 25:11 we read, *"A word fitly spoken [is like] apples of gold in pictures of silver."* Joel places the tree among the other fruitful trees of the field such as the vine, the fig tree, the pomegranate and the palm (1:12). The latter represent the joy of the sons of men.

This description of the apple tree suggests that it is, in fact, the apricot rather than the apple or quince. The apricot flourishes in the highlands and lowlands alike. Its size and pale foliage give a refreshing shade, while the fruit is golden, sweet and exudes a sweet perfume.

If we put these ideas together, we find Christ as the Glorious One who gives *joy, shelter, comfort, fruit and fragrance.* Firstly, there is **joy**. In John 15:11 the Lord Jesus says: *"These things have I spoken unto you, that my joy might remain in you, and [that] your joy might be full."* These fitly spoken words which the Lord had addressed to His disciples had prepared them with facts, teaching and promises for His absence. As *friends* they were informed as to why He had to leave them. As *disciples* they were instructed as to their behaviour and obedience. The result was that they were able to share in His joy, and that their joy be full or complete. 'Joy' means the same as 'delight'. Knowing the Lord we have a deep-seated joy in our hearts that cannot be touched by circumstances. It is constant because of the certainty of His work and promises. However, our happiness tends to relate to the circumstances of life. Our joy prevents things becoming too burdensome. It is a safety valve. Like the apostle Paul we can say that we may be troubled about things, but not distressed. We may be perplexed, but not in despair. So may we be persecuted, yet not forsaken. We may even be cast down, but not destroyed (See 2 Corinthians 4:8-9).

In John 17:13, Jesus says, *"And now come I to thee; and these things I speak in the world, that they might have my joy fulfilled in themselves."* One of the reasons for this prayer of the Son of God to the Father was in order that His joy might be fulfilled in the disciples. It was His delight to do the will of His Father. It was His joy to look past the cross to the fulfilment of every counsel and purpose of God. Yet, both depended on His death upon the tree at Golgotha.

Secondly, there is **shelter** from the heat of the sun. The latter, comparing Matthew 13:6 and 21, is symbolic of tribulation or persecution. By sitting under His shadow, we are sheltered from the full force of both. Yet, the "tree" itself suffers the brunt of that heat. *"For in that he himself hath suffered being tempted, he is able to succour them that are tempted"* (Hebrews 2:18). *"For we have not an high priest which cannot be touched with the feeling of our infirmities; but was in all points tempted like as [we are, yet] without sin"* (Hebrews 4:15).

Nevertheless, we do suffer. We are tried, but 1 Corinthians 10:13 states: *"There hath no temptation (trial) taken you but such as is common to man: but God [is] faithful, who will not suffer you to be tempted above that ye are able; but will with the temptation also make a way of escape, that ye may be able to bear [it]."* The way of escape from trial is to obey God's word during it. His guidance leads to the gateway of peace.

Thirdly, He is able to provide **comfort and support**. He is the Lord. Underneath are the everlasting arms. He has promised never to leave or to forsake us. He is our Great High Priest who sighs with our sighs whether in trial, sorrow or affliction. The Psalmists knew the comfort and support of the Lord. In Psalm 86:17 we read, *"...Because* *thou, LORD, hast holpen me, and comforted me."* In Psalm 23 there is reference to the Shepherd restoring the soul of David and His rod and staff being a comfort to him. Isaiah 49:13 states, *"Sing, O heavens; and be joyful, O earth; and break forth into singing, O mountains: for the LORD hath comforted his people, and will have mercy upon his afflicted."* Then, in verse 16 the LORD speaks to Zion, *"Behold, I have graven thee upon the palms of [my] hands; thy walls [are] continually before me."*

We are comforted to know that Christ appears in the presence of God for us. He pleads our cause. He intercedes on our behalf. He is our Advocate (Comforter) indeed – one who restores our souls when we sin. And, besides this, He has given the Holy Spirit to indwell us. *"But the Comforter, [which is] the Holy Ghost, whom the Father will send in my name, he shall teach you all things, and bring all things to your remembrance, whatsoever I have said unto you"* (John 14:26). Hence, we have two Comforters of the same kind – the Holy Spirit and the Son of God! How wonderfully God provides for His children!!

Furthermore, the Lord Jesus asked His disciples to pray for Israel in a coming day of trouble. In the middle of the seven years of great tribulation that will come upon the earth, Israel's faithful will be persecuted (Matthew 24:15-22). They will flee for refuge. The Lord asked that prayer be made that their flight be not in winter or on the Sabbath day (verse 20). He also expresses His concerns for those who are with child or giving suck to babies (verse 19). Therefore, the prayer would be that few would be pregnant or feeding tiny ones at that time.

His **fruit** is sweet to the taste. The Lord Jesus Christ was led by the Spirit in every aspect of His life. A life uniquely marked by the fruit of the Spirit (Galatians 5:22). Love was the pinnacle of that fruit. Love, joy, peace, longsuffering, gentleness, goodness, faith, meekness and temperance were the marks of the devoted and dependent Man.

The **fragrance** of Christ rises to God as a sweet smell, whether it is the beauty of His devoted life or the perfection of His sacrifice.

4. THE COMPARISON

The force of the comparison suggests that Christ is preeminent above all the excellent of Israel. We might say that He is the Excellent of the excellent. In Him we find all the blessing of the Lord. We are blessed with all spiritual blessings in the heavenlies in Christ Jesus. He is the One who protects and supports. He is the One who gives joy. He is the One whom having not seen, we love; in whom, though now we do not see Him, yet believing, we rejoice with joy unspeakable and full of glory. There is nobody as noble as He!

There have been many kings in Israel and in Judah, but Christ is the King of kings and Lord of lords. We may determine this from Hebrews 1:8-9 where we read, *"But unto the Son [he saith], Thy throne, O God, [is] for ever and ever: a sceptre of righteousness [is] the sceptre of thy kingdom. Thou hast loved righteousness and hated iniquity; therefore God, [even] thy God, hath anointed thee with the oil of gladness above thy fellows."*

It may be worth noting that prophet, priest and king were all subjected to anointing. We have seen that Christ is the King of kings; but is there any prophet who is able to match Christ? The woman of Samaria said, *"Sir, I perceive that thou art a prophet"* (John 4:19). He is the Prophet predicted in Deuteronomy 18:18: *"I will raise them up a Prophet from among their brethren, like unto thee, and will put my words in his mouth; and he shall speak unto them all that I shall command him."* Was there ever a high priest that could be called "great" as is our Lord? *"Seeing then that we have a great high priest, that is passed into the heavens, Jesus the Son of God, let us hold fast [our] profession"* (Hebrews 4:14).

We also find that the word "firstborn" or "first-begotten" meaning position, honour, rank or dignity is used of Christ. In Colossians 1:15, He, the Son of the Father's love, is the firstborn of every creature or, better, "all creation". That is to say, He ever was pre-eminent even before creation and He Himself produced creation. In verse 18, we are taught that in all things He might have the pre-eminence. Here He is called the firstborn from among the dead. He has pre-eminence in resurrection itself because His life and Person demanded it. Whereas, the resurrection of others depends on the mercy of God.

In Romans 8:29, He is the firstborn of many brethren. This means that He, the Son of God, is the Chief or Unique One of every member of God's family. He is the Son over His own house. In Hebrews 1:6, He, the Son, is the firstborn whom God again brings into the world. He is the One whom all the angels of God were allowed to worship. So he is greater than angels. This speaks, particularly, of His place when He appears in glory. He will be Supreme and everyone will bow to Him. In Revelation 1:5, He, Jesus Christ, is the firstborn of the dead. He is the Greatest One of all those who are raised from the dead.

So, whether we are comparing Christ to kings, priests, prophets, creation, resurrection, resurrected ones or brethren – He is far above them all – Supreme! Glory to His name!

Chapter Four
The Roe or Young Hart

"My beloved is like a roe or young hart: behold, he standeth behind our wall, he looketh forth at the windows, shewing himself through the lattice." (Song 2:9)

In this section, we will examine:

1. how Christ is like a roe or young hart;

2. why He takes up the position behind the wall; and,

3. the reason behind His action of shewing Himself through the lattice.

1. CHRIST LIKENED TO A ROE OR YOUNG HART

The roe and young hart both belong to the deer family. Many believe that the roe speaks of the gazelle. Their characteristics are noted in Scripture where they are:

   a. used for food (Deuteronomy 12:15, 22; 14:5; 15:22 and 1 Kings 4:23);

   b. noted for their speed and ability to leap (2 Samuel 2:18; 1 Chronicles 12:8; Song 2:17; Isaiah 35:6);

   c. alert to danger (Proverbs 6:5);

   d. pleasant (Proverbs 5:19; Song 2:9);

e. often panting after the water-brooks (Psalm 42:1); and,

f. a sign of provision in a time of prosperity (1 Kings 4:23).

A. USED FOR FOOD

As the animal is used for food, we find it is classed as clean by God. This reminds us of the purity of our Lord Jesus Christ. He did no sin. He knew no sin. There was no sin in Him. It must be realised that even though Christ was tested by the devil in the wilderness in the aspects of spirit, soul and body, it was impossible for Him to sin because He was God the Son. He went through the temptations in order to show us how godly men should respond to the devil in similar circumstances, namely, we are to use the Word of God to resist Satan's attacks.

In the New Testament (John 6) we find Christ declaring Himself to be:

- the "True Bread" unveiling Himself as the antitype of the manna which came down from heaven – He was the genuine article, the real food for His people (verse 32);

- the "Bread of God" telling of the One whose authority was of God and who gives life to the world (verse 33);

- the "Bread of life" – the I AM (Yahweh) who is able to give to men everlasting life (verse 48);

- the "Bread from Heaven" showing the original place of His being (verse 50); and,

- the "Living Bread" revealing the eternity of His being (verse 51).

In verses 51 and 53, we find the words *"…if any one shall have eaten"* (N.Tr.) and *"…unless ye shall have eaten"* (N.Tr.). These words are in figurative language speaking of initial faith in Christ, the living bread. That faith results in the possession of eternal life. By believing on Christ, the living bread, we have everlasting life (verses 47-48). This was the purpose of John in writing this gospel: *"…That ye might believe that Jesus is the Christ, the Son of God; and that believing ye might have life through his name"* (John 20:31).

Jesus went on to use the same idea of eating and drinking in verses 54, 56, 57 and 58. Here it refers to an ongoing eating and drinking. It means that we should continue to apprehend Him more and more by faith. We are to grow in grace and in the knowledge of Jesus Christ our Lord. The first epistle of John ends with the words: *"And we know that the Son of God is come, and hath given us an understanding, that we may know him that is true, and we are in him that is true, [even] in his Son Jesus Christ. This is the true God and eternal life"* (5:20).

In verse 63 of John chapter 6, Jesus shows that these words are spirit and life. That is to say, they are not to be taken literally. So we are not to relate them to the Lord's

Supper. The terminology does *not* indicate that the bread and wine change into the flesh and blood of Christ.

B. SPEED AND AGILITY

Both here in Song 2:8 and in 2:17, we find the coming of the beloved likened to that of the hart or roe upon the mountains and upon the hills. As the beloved approaches, he is said to leap upon the mountains and skip upon the hills. That is to say, no distance is too great and no hindrance is too stubborn to prevent him coming with joy in his step.

If we apply this to our personal lives as Christians, then the mountains of unbelief, carnality and worldliness will not prevent Him seeking to have fellowship with us. What was true for Israel was true for each one of us: *"But your iniquities have separated between you and your God, and your sins have hid [his] face from you"* (Isaiah 59:2). However, if we confess our sin, God is faithful and just to forgive us our sin and to cleanse us from all unrighteousness (1 John 1:9). Why? It was because Christ was made sin on our account. He has also borne our sins in His own body on the tree. The desire of Christ is that we should have part with Him and to be with Him where He is, therefore, He washes us by the washing of water by the word (Ephesians 5:26).

When the Lord Jesus returns to Zion (read: Isaiah chapters 60–62), every difficulty which has been set up will be nothing to Him. He is able to overcome every barrier. His coming will be at the speed and with the brightness of lightning (Matthew 24:27) and the enemies of Israel will be destroyed. Zion shall be a crown of glory in the hand of the LORD, and a royal diadem in the hand of her God. She will not be termed 'Forsaken' any longer, nor shall her land be 'Desolate'; but she shall be called *Hephzibah* 'in

whom is my delight' and her land *Beulah* 'married' or
'inhabited' because Yahweh delights in her. The land shall
be married! (Isaiah 62:3-4). Both the land and the people
are grasped by the plans of Yahweh. In his book on Isaiah,
William Kelly states that this will be the basis of patriot-
ism in Israel [1] because verse 5 goes on to say: *"For [as] a
young man marrieth a virgin, shall thy sons marry thee; and
with the joy of the bridegroom over the bride, shall thy God
rejoice over thee"* (N.Tr.).

When the Lord Jesus comes for the church, He Himself
will come into the air – the very domain of Satan who is
called the prince of the power of the air. The devil and his
hordes will be powerless to prevent Christ from snatching
away His people. He will not be prevented. *"He which tes-
tifieth these things saith, Surely I come quickly. Amen. Even
so, come, Lord Jesus"* (Revelation 22:20).

C. ALERT TO DANGER

In Proverbs 6:5 we read: *"Deliver thyself as a roe from the
hand [of the hunter]… "*. There is a hunter who seeks out
to ensnare the godly. 2 Corinthians 11:14 states, *"…for
Satan himself is transformed into an angel of light."* Here
Satan is seen as the adversary of the godly and seeks to
trap them by using false teaching. As we have seen already,
the devil took this character when he dared tempt the Son
of God Himself in Luke 4:1-13. Satan tested Christ in
spirit (verses 9-12), soul (verses 5-8) and body (verses 2-
4). He used the scriptures improperly as a net. Christ
defeated him by the proper use of scripture. So Christ was
tempted in all points as we are, yet without sin (Hebrews
2:18). What an example He is to us!

1 Peter 5:8 states, *"Be sober; be vigilant; because your adversary the devil, as a roaring lion, walketh about, seeking*

---

[1] William Kelly *An Exposition of the Book of Isaiah*, new edition, p 457

whom he may devour." Again we see the devil, or accuser of the godly, in a more vicious form, namely one which uses violent means to ruin God's children. This may take the form of persecution. In the life of Christ, we can see this in the way He was abused by Jew and Gentile alike. He suffered at the hand of man for righteousness' sake. Yet behind the scenes, we find the devil. In Psalm 22, which so clearly speaks of the cross of Christ, we see the hind of the morning (Aijeleth Shahar) being attacked by the strong ones of Bashan who gaped upon Him with their mouths as a ravening and roaring lion. He was persecuted by those who, driven by envy, opposed Him. These were the Jewish leaders of the day. Furthermore, He was surrounded by "dogs". The latter represent the Gentiles. It was "the assembly of the wicked" that pierced His hands and His feet. In it all, He remained faithful to God – *"My God, my God..."* (Mark 15:34); He was forgiving – *"Father forgive them..."* (Luke 23:34); He cared for His own – *"Woman, behold thy son!...Behold thy mother!"* (John 19:26-27); and He fulfilled the scriptures – *"I thirst"* (John 19:28).

The Seven Words From The Cross

The cross, 'tis there we hear Love's voice
Its perfect utterings cry;
While men with scoffing loud and rude
Deridingly passed by.

"Father, forgive them," was Thy prayer,
"They know not what they do."
Casting lots upon Thy vesture
Soldiers reviled Thee too.

The one whom Thou didst love was there;
Thy wounded mother see;
"Woman, behold thy son," was breathed:
And, "This thy mother be."

One thief, with venom, railed on Thee,
The other saw Thy worth;
"Today, shalt Thou with me be
In paradise" burst forth.

'Twas then that dreadful sound rang out –
From out of darkness deep:
"My God, why'st Thou forsaken Me!"
Sin's distance Thou didst reap.

With parched throat, Thou, Saviour sighed
With quiet voice, "I thirst."
And so the Scripture was fulfilled.
Thy Father's will came first.

The silent hours called out in love,
While judgment raked Thy heart:
"Finished, it is!" and loud the shout;
Now we with Thee have part.

Thou saith, "Father, into Thy hands,
My spirit I commend."
Thou bow'st Thy head, gave up the ghost,
And there Thy sufferings end.

(G. E. Stevens)

The first Adam failed under the deception of the Serpent, but the last Adam overcame that enemy of God. Now He is the Leader of a new race, a race of those who have trusted in Him. Soon, He will have dominion over this world – the dominion the first Adam lost.

Oh that we might be alert to danger in the same way! 1 John 2:14-16 warn us all, *"I have written unto you, fathers, because ye have known him [that is] from the beginning. I have written unto you, young men, because ye are strong, and the word of God abideth in you, and ye have overcome the wicked one. Love not the world, neither the things [that are] in the world. If any man love the world, the love of the Father is not in him. For all that [is] in the world, the lust of the flesh, and the lust of the eyes, and the pride of life, is not of the Father, but is of the world."* If we love the Father, we will do the will of God (verse 17).

In the context of the scripture "love not the world" refers to a system of mankind that is in direct opposition to God. The fads, fashions and opinions of this system are contrary, even hostile, to the mind of God. James 4:4 shows that a believer who loves the world is a traitor: *"Ye… adulteresses, know ye not that the friendship of the world is enmity with God? whosoever therefore will be a friend of the world is the enemy of God."*

The world is marked by:

- the lust of the flesh – the strong desires of our fallen, sinful nature leading to constant temptation from within;

- the lust of the eyes – the strong desire produced within to possess or be influenced by that which is without;

- the pride of life is a reliance upon one's own ability seeking honour from others.

These three aspects led Eve to succumb to the temptation of the serpent in Genesis chapter 3. In Luke chapter 4, we see Jesus triumphant when He was tempted by the devil in these three areas. In His hunger, He was asked to indulge Himself by changing stones into bread – *the lust of the flesh.* In His condition of poverty He was asked to exalt Himself accepting the displayed kingdoms of the world as His own – *the lust of the eyes*. The temptation to throw Himself from the pinnacle of the temple was asking Him to display Himself before others in order to prove Himself to be the Son of God – *the pride of life*. Christ answered every temptation of the devil by quoting words of Deuteronomy. He was alert to the wiles of the devil. He would not use His power for His own benefit. Let us also resist the devil and he will flee from us.

D. PLEASANT (PROVERBS 5:19; SONG 2:9)

In Proverbs 5:19 we see the desire of Solomon for the wife of a man's youth. She was to be as a loving hind and pleasant roe. Her breasts were to satisfy her husband at all times and he was to be continually ravished by her love. So we can see that there is a relationship of love expressed here. This we see in the sacrificial love of Christ.

- The Son of God who loved me and gave himself for *me* (Galatians 2:20).

- Christ loved us and gave himself for *us* (Ephesians 5:2).

- Christ also loved the church and gave himself for *it* (Ephesians 5:25).

The Hebrew word for 'pleasant' in Proverbs 5:19 may be translated as 'grace'. The Son of God was full of grace and truth (John 1:14). In 2 Corinthians 8:9 we read, *"For ye know the grace of our Lord Jesus Christ, that though he was rich, yet for your sakes he became poor, that ye through his poverty might be rich."* GRACE has been said to be **G**od's **R**edemption **A**t **C**hrist's **E**xpense. It is the sovereign favour of God flowing out to sinful man on the one hand and to the saint of God on the other. It is by grace we are saved through faith (Ephesians 2:8), but grace also sustains the believer through life (2 Corinthians 12:9).

In Isaiah 60:10, the LORD's favour is linked with mercy. Mercy and truth, and righteousness and peace all met together in the sacrifice of Christ. One day, the people of Israel will look upon Him whom they pierced. Recognising what they did to their Messiah, they shall mourn.

In Luke 2:52, we find the development of Jesus in intelligence, in physique, in spirit and socially: *"And Jesus increased in wisdom and stature, and in favour with God and man."*

E. PANTING AFTER THE WATER-BROOKS (PSALM 42:1)

Although roes and harts are normally ruminants, they hate snakes. Historians, such as Pliny, have recorded that given the opportunity, they will trample them, tear them in pieces and eat them. After feeding, the roe becomes extremely thirsty. However, instinct tells them that they cannot drink until the snakes are digested. They have to forbear. This often results in dreadful cries and violent pantings.

This reminds us of Christ as the One who has defeated that old serpent, the devil. In Genesis 3:15 God promised that the Seed of the woman (Christ) would bruise the head of the Serpent's seed (unbelievers) in a future day. The language is fitting for the roe who tramples the serpent – *"He shall bruise thy head, and thou shalt bruise his heel"*. Hebrews 2:14-15 speak of the devil's defeat: *"Forasmuch then as the children are partakers of flesh and blood, he also himself likewise took part of the same; that through death he might destroy him that had the power of death, the devil; and deliver them who through fear of death were all their lifetime subject to bondage."* Death has been defeated by the Son of God. He is risen! The devil is disarmed!

In a future day, Satan will be bound for a thousand years while Christ reigns over the earth. Finally, the devil will be cast into the lake of fire that burns with brimstone. There he will be tormented day and night for ever (Revelation 20:10). There are two options open to people today. The first is to spend eternity with Christ in glory. The second is to spend eternity with the devil in torment. Believe in the Lord Jesus Christ and you shall be saved!

In passing, it is worthy of note that the roe has longevity of life. Alexander the Great once took some of them and placed gold chains about their necks. Some were recovered a hundred years later with the chains enveloped by fat about their necks. It reminds us that Christ lives after the power of an endless life. He could say, *"I [am] he that liveth, and was dead; and, behold, I am alive for evermore, Amen; and have the keys of hell (hades) and of death"* (Revelation 1:18).

> *His be the Victor's name,*
> *Who fought the fight alone.*
> *Triumphant saints no honour claim,*
> *His conquest was their own.*
>
> *By weakness and defeat,*
> *He won the meed and crown;*
> *Trod all our foes beneath His feet,*
> *By being trodden down.*
>
> (S. W. Gandy)

F. A SIGN OF PROVISION IN A TIME OF PROSPERITY (1 KINGS 4:22-24)

In 1 Kings 4:22-24, we read: *"And Solomon's provision for one day was thirty measures of fine flour, and threescore measures of meal, ten fat oxen, and twenty oxen out of the pastures, and an hundred sheep, beside harts, and roebucks, and fallow deer, and fatted fowl. For he had dominion over*

*all [the region] on this side the river, from Tiphsah even to
Azzah, over all the kings on this side the river: and he had
peace on all sides round about him."*

The sustenance of Solomon's household for one day
included harts and gazelles. In other words, there was a
plentiful supply of food. God was blessing this man. He
had dominion. Peace reigned. The people dwelt in safety.
What a day of blessing!

Taking Solomon as typical of the King of kings and Lord
of lords, even our Lord Jesus Christ, we see that all these
things will mark His reign. It is a reign that will last for a
thousand years. If Solomon in all his glory was not
clothed as beautifully as the lily of the field, that of Christ
will be far greater – after all, He created the flower. A peek
into His future glory was seen on the Mount of
Transfiguration: *"And he was transfigured before them. And
his face shone as the sun, and his garments became white as
the light..."* (Matthew 17:2, N.Tr.).

Psalm 72 is Messianic. It describes the rule of Christ as
follows (N.Tr.):

verses 1-7: The Character of His Rule:

*O God, give the king thy judgements, and thy righteousness
unto the king's son. He will judge thy people with righteousness, and thine afflicted with judgement. The mountains
shall bring peace to the people, and the hills, by righteousness.
He will do justice to the afflicted of the people; he will save
the children of the needy, and will break in pieces the oppres-
sor. They shall fear thee as long as sun and moon endure, from
generation to generation. He shall come down like rain on the
mown grass, as showers that water the earth. In his days shall
the righteous flourish, and abundance of peace till the moon
be no more.*

69

verses 8-10: The Extent of His Rule:

And he shall have dominion from sea to sea, and from the river unto the ends of the earth. The dwellers in the desert shall bow before him, and his enemies shall lick the dust. The kings of Tarshish and of the isles shall render presents; the kings of Sheba and Seba shall offer tribute.

verses 11-16: The Comfort of His Rule:

Yea, all kings shall bow down before him; all nations shall serve him. For he will deliver the needy who crieth, and the afflicted, who hath no helper; He will have compassion on the poor and needy, and will save the souls of the needy: He will redeem their souls from oppression and violence, and precious shall their blood be in his sight. And he shall live; and to him shall be given of the gold of Sheba; and prayer shall be made for him continually: all the day shall he be blessed. There shall be abundance of corn in the earth, upon the top of the mountains; the fruit thereof shall shake like Lebanon; and they of the city shall bloom like the herb of the earth.

verse 17: The Joy of His Rule:

His name shall endure for ever; his name shall be continued as long as the sun: and [men] shall bless themselves in him; all nations shall call him blessed.

verse 18: The Blessing Resulting from His Rule:

Blessed be Jehovah (Yahweh) *Elohim, the God of Israel, who alone doeth wondrous things! And blessed be his glorious name for ever! and let the whole earth be filled with his glory! Amen, and Amen. The prayers of David the son of Jesse are ended.*

So Solomon's reign is merely a picture of a great reign to come. Daniel 2 speaks of a stone cut out of the mountain without hands that represents a kingdom that destroys every other and stands for ever. Daniel is predicting the millennial reign of Christ. The initial scope of that reign is shown on Map 1 – Page 81 – and may be confirmed by reading Ezekiel chapters 47 & 48. Yet, that reign will extend eastwards as far as the River Euphrates during the period of the millennium so that the prophecies given to Abraham (Genesis 15:18) and to Moses (Deuteronomy 11:24) will be fulfilled.

In Isaiah 11, we find a further indication of the character of the King and His kingdom: *"And there shall come forth a rod out of the stem of Jesse, and a Branch shall grow out of his roots: and the spirit of the LORD shall rest upon him, the spirit of wisdom and understanding, the spirit of counsel and might, the spirit of knowledge and of the fear of the LORD; and shall make him of quick understanding in the fear of the LORD: and he shall not judge after the sight of his eyes, neither reprove after the hearing of his ears: but with righteousness shall he judge the poor, and reprove with equity for the meek of the earth: and he shall smite the earth with the rod of his mouth, and with the breath of his lips shall he slay the wicked. And righteousness shall be the girdle of his loins, and faithfulness the girdle of his reins.*

The wolf also shall dwell with the lamb, and the leopard shall lie down with the kid; and the calf and the young lion and the fatling together; and a little child shall lead them. And the cow and the bear shall feed; their young ones shall lie down together: and the lion shall eat straw like the ox. And the sucking child shall play on the hole of the asp, and the weaned child shall put his hand on the cockatrice' den. They shall not hurt nor destroy in all my holy mountain: for the earth shall be full of the knowledge of the LORD, as the waters cover the sea.

And in that day there shall be a root of Jesse, which shall stand for an ensign of the people; to it shall the Gentiles seek: and his rest shall be glorious" (Isaiah 11:1-10).

The verses above indicate the moral worth of the Messiah as already discussed. It then describes the character of His kingdom. Both Israel and the Gentiles will be blessed in that glorious day. The fact that a shoot or rod comes from the stem of Jesse indicates that from a lowly and, in the long term, unsuccessful royal line will arise the Messiah – David's greater Son. The Deliverer shall come out of Zion and turn away ungodliness from Jacob. The lawless or wicked one (Antichrist) is destroyed by the brightness of His coming (2 Thessalonians 2:8). All things will be gathered together in Christ. Even the animals of creation will be at peace with one another when the Prince of Peace reigns. As Romans 8:21-22 state: *"… The creature itself also shall be delivered from the bondage of corruption into the glorious liberty of the children of God. For we know that the whole creation groaneth and travaileth in pain together until now"*.

In Revelation 11:15 we are told that the kingdoms of this world become the kingdom of our Lord, and of His Christ; and He shall reign for ever and ever. In chapter 20 we read of Satan being bound for a thousand years and of the tribulation martyrs living and reigning with Christ for a thousand years. At the end of that time, Satan will be released and men shall once again rise against the Lord and His anointed. They are destroyed with fire from heaven. The beast, false prophet and the devil will all be found in the lake of fire and brimstone, namely, Hell. The Son of God then hands the kingdom back to God the Father (1 Corinthians 15:24).

Ezekiel chapters 45 and 48 outline the structures of the new temple and the city of Jerusalem for that thousand years reign of Christ (see Diagram 2 – Page 83). The Bible mentions five temples relative to Israel:

- Solomon's Temple;
- Zerubbabel's Temple;
- Herod's Temple;
- Jews' Temple; and,
- Millennial Temple.

Every part of Solomon's temple uttered the glory of God. Unfortunately, the people turned to idolatry and God allowed Nebuchadnezzar to sack Jerusalem and loot and burn the temple (2 Chronicles 36:19).

Years later, God put it into the mind of Zerubbabel to rebuild the temple. However, the glory of that temple lacked the wonderful beauty of the original. The latter was enlarged and beautified by Herod, but not by God-given instructions. Herod's temple was completely destroyed in AD 70 by the armies of the Roman general, Titus – so fulfilling the prophecy of the Lord Jesus in Luke 21:5-6.

The next temple to be built will be the Jews' temple. It must be constructed about the start of the Great Tribulation period because the abomination of desolation will be set up in it at the central point of the seven years appointed in Daniel 9. Compare Daniel 9:27 and Matthew 24:15. This abomination is the raising up of the image of the "beast" by the Antichrist (Daniel 12:11; Revelation 13:14-15). This temple will be built in unbelief, possibly for political reasons.

Today, we see the Palestinian Arab and Israel locked in a cycle of violence resulting from terrorist attacks upon Israel. The Mosque of Omar (Dome of the Rock) stands on the sacred temple site a crowning monument to Islam. Should this mosque be removed by the Israelis, then the whole of the Islamic world would rise up in arms and, in the present political climate, so would other nations. Hence, it has been rumoured this temple will be built upon the Mount of Olives instead. However, if this temple is to be built upon Mount Moriah, then God Himself or the Moslems themselves will have to act to cleanse the present site. Such an act would confirm Israel to be the chosen people of God. It is equally difficult to see this happening because it would bring faith to Israel prematurely.

Nevertheless, it was noteworthy that the November 2004 issue of the magazine *Israel Today* contained an article entitled "Ramadan Sparks New Temple Mount Dispute". The article expressed fears that the weight of thousands of worshippers visiting the two mosques on the site (the Al-Aqsa Mosque and the Dome of the Rock) might cause it to collapse. The cause of this concern is stated as follows: "Israeli archaeologists and engineers charge that unauthorised Moslem construction of an underground mosque in Solomon's Stables has weakened the foundation of the Temple Mount. A bulge and cracks have already appeared on the southern wall of the compound, a possible omen of disaster." The report continues by saying that the situation was made more acute following an earthquake (5 on the Richter Scale) in the area only a few months previously.

Interestingly, a leading Jewish Rabbi outlined the conditions for the building of the temple in an article in *The Jerusalem Post*, 20th April, 1988. They included:

- the land of Israel being delivered from foreign domination;

- the establishment of a sovereign Jewish government;

- an ingathering of exiles that would result in a Jewish majority in the land and its settlement;

- the establishment of a Sanhedrin; and, of course,

- the rebuilding of the temple.

From these conditions we can readily assume in 2009, that the plans and even the materials have been prepared for the construction of this temple.

The future temple (as revealed by Ezekiel) will be built following major topographical changes when the Lord Jesus Christ appears. An example of this is seen in Zechariah 14:4 when Christ shall stand upon the Mount of Olives which then parts to the west and east forming a "very great valley" running north-south. Verse 8 of the same chapter describes waters flowing out from Jerusalem in two directions: a river flowing to the Mediterranean Sea and another flowing to the Dead Sea.

The Millennial Temple will be God's dwelling place on earth. Hence, Jerusalem shall be named "Yahweh-Shammah" meaning, "the Lord is there". Jeremiah 3:17 and Zechariah 2:10-12 reveal this to be so: *"At that time they shall call Jerusalem the throne of the LORD; and all the nations shall be gathered unto it, to the name of the LORD, to Jerusalem: neither shall they walk any more after the imagination of their evil heart"* (Jeremiah 3:17).

"Sing and rejoice, O daughter of Zion: for, lo, I come, and I will dwell in the midst of thee, saith the LORD. And many nations shall be joined to the LORD in that day, and shall be my people: and I will dwell in the midst of thee, and thou shalt know that the LORD of hosts hath sent me unto thee. And the LORD shall inherit Judah his portion in the holy

land, and shall choose Jerusalem again" (Zechariah 2:10-12).

The temple is described in Ezekiel chapters 41-47. The first part of the temple mentioned in Ezekiel 40 is the wall. A wall protects. The gate mentioned next speaks of entry by the right way. The chambers show that there is room for the priests to dwell in God's presence in order to serve the Lord in the temple. This means that Israel's priesthood will be revived. No doubt, the genealogy of the priests will be made clear by God. The fact that offerings will be slain and offered shows that Israel will remember what happened to their Messiah at His first advent and know their own imperfections even as the people of God. In chapters 41 and 42 we find the most holy place described. This is the central place of God's dwelling. The many chambers were for the priests. The whole sanctuary is measured as just over one square mile.

Chapter 43 outlines the way in which the glory of the Lord filled the house. God once again dwells in the midst of His earthly people. The altar speaks of the sacrifice of Christ for the acceptance of the people of God. Christ is seen as the One made sin in the sin offering, while His perfections and the joy of communion are seen in the burnt and peace offerings respectively.

In chapters 44-46, the east gate is to be shut because the Lord had entered by it. None other was to have that privilege. The "prince" is then introduced. This prince will be of the tribe of Judah from which the sceptre will not depart. *"My servant David [shall be] their prince for ever"* (Ezekiel 37:25). This prince is *not* the Lord as some think because he eats bread before the Lord; he enters by the porch of the east gate; he has a particular segment of land for his possession; and he prepares a sin offering for *himself* and for the people at the time of the Passover.

Chapter 47 tells us of a stream of water flowing from the altar, under the threshold of the house towards the east. It then turns towards the south. It soon grows into an ever-deepening river. It carries healing in its flow. By its banks grow many trees whose leaf does not fade, nor is their fruit consumed. The fruit will become a constant supply of food and the leaf a source of medicine. It flows through Jerusalem and splits into two. One section flowing to the Mediterranean. The other, flowing to the Dead Sea, brings life with it (Ezekiel 47:9-10).

The river indicates that all will not be perfect in the millennial period. If there is need for medicine, then there is still a degree of sickness. Nevertheless, it shows the greatness of God's blessing and it all begins with that which represents the offering of Christ who by the eternal Spirit offered Himself without spot unto God: the altar. Although an actual river, we know from other scriptures (e.g. John 7:38) that flowing water is symbolic of the Holy Spirit of God. It is this Spirit who brings life and blessing.

2. THE POSITION BEHIND THE WALL

The wall represents a variety of aspects in the Scriptures including: defence (Nehemiah 4:13), possession (Leviticus 25:31) and separation (Ephesians 2:14). Would the Lord leap the defences of the bride? Would He seek to claim her possessions? Would they remain separate? The Lord waits to be invited in. It reminds us of Revelation 3:20: *"Behold, I stand at the door, and knock: if any man hear my voice, and open the door, I will come in to him, and will sup with him, and he with me."* This is pure grace! The wall of the Law of Moses now has in it a door marked Grace! It is Love – the Royal Law. Jesus said, *"If a man love me, he will keep my words: and my Father will love him, and we will come unto him, and make our abode with him"* (John 14:23).

3. SHEWING HIMSELF THROUGH THE LATTICE

He looks for his girlfriend through the windows. "Shewing himself" actually means "glancing suddenly and stealthily" through the lattice. He is being careful – remaining alert. Enemies could be nearby.

The Scriptures give us glimpses of Christ through a lattice. The Lord Jesus spoke to the two disciples on the Emmaus road, saying: *"O fools, and slow of heart to believe all that the prophets have spoken: ought not Christ to have suffered these things, and to enter into his glory? And beginning at Moses and all the prophets, he expounded unto them in all the scriptures the things concerning himself"* (Luke 24:25-27).

A simplified division of the Scriptures reveals the following:

- Figures of Christ in the Pentateuch;

- Foretellings of Christ in the Prophets;

- Feelings of Christ in the Poetry;

- Facts of Christ in the Gospels;

- Fame of Christ in the Acts;

- Fruit of Christ in the Epistles; and,

- Finality of Christ in the Revelation.

So, Christ is only seen by faith, through the window of God's Word (Luke 24:35; John 14:21); yet we do not have full vision. 1 Corinthians 13:12 states: *"For now we see through a glass, darkly; but then face to face: now I know in part; but then shall I know even as also I am known."* This gives us an incentive to look for His appearing (Isaiah 33:17; Titus 2:13).

Son of man

1.

Son of man, in heav'n we view Thee,
Sitting now at God's right hand,
Waiting for that day of glory
When Thy rod shall rule the land.
O the brightness of the splendour
Of our great God, Lord and King;
O the glory of our Saviour,
Jesus Christ, of whom we sing!

2.

Son of man, the pain of sorrows,
Falls upon this groaning earth;
Famines, wars and other horrors –
Rage and swell to quench Man's mirth.
O the wonder of Thy Person,
Thou, the Son and Heir of all;
Thou the impress of God's image,
Loved by those Thou cam'st to call.

3.

Son of man, Thy sign in heaven –
Flashing lightning from the east;
Speed and light with power and glory
Put down foes both great and least.
O the marvel of our Maker,
Thou the One whose word upholds,
Heaven's best, our well-Beloved,
Who the Father's will unfolds!

4.

Son of man, Thou shalt have honour
In the world that caused Thee pain —
Men shall know that Thou hast loved us
When Thy wife with Thee shall reign.
O the beauty of the Bridegroom!
King and Priest upon Thy throne.
Servant, Man and Lord of glory
Worthy is Thy name alone!

(G. E. Stevens)

Map 1:

The Approximate Millennial Division of the Land of Israel (Ezekiel 47 & 48)

THE MILLENIAL DIVISIONS
OF THE LAND OF ISRAEL
EZEKIEL 47 & 48

HAMATH

The Way to Hethlon

Zedad

Hamath   Lebo-Hamath   Hazar-Enon

Berothan   DAN

ASHER   Sibraim

THE GREAT SEA

(THE MEDITERRANEAN)

NAPHTALI

Damascus

EPHRAIM

HAURAN

REUBEN

Hazar-Hatican

SEA OF GALILEE

JUDAH

LEVITES' PART

GILEAD

PRIESTS' PART

River Jordan

CITY/SUBURBS
Jerusalem

BENJAMIN

EASTERN SEA
(DEAD SEA)

SIMEON

ISSACHAR

Brook of Egypt

ZEBULON   Tamar

Kadesh-Barneah   GAD

(NB: The above map is based on one reed = 10ft. 6ins. It is difficult to tell whether the priests' part was north of the Levites' or central. It has been placed centrally because the sanctuary is "in the midst" of the 25000 reed square and also "in the midst" of the priests' part. Furthermore, the city section is said to be next to the holy section in Ezekiel 48:18).

DIAGRAM 1:

THE HEAVE OFFERING OF THE LAND (INCLUDING THE LEVITES', PRIESTS' AND PRINCE'S SECTIONS)

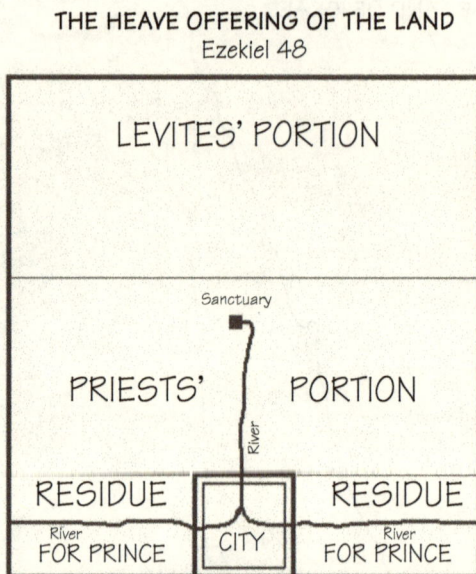

THE HEAVE OFFERING OF THE LAND
Ezekiel 48

LEVITES' PORTION

Sanctuary

PRIESTS'   PORTION

River

RESIDUE   RESIDUE

River
FOR PRINCE   CITY   River
FOR PRINCE

DIAGRAM 2:

THE MILLENNIAL TEMPLE (ACCORDING TO EZEKIEL 40-43)

THE MILLENNIAL TEMPLE
(Dimensions are in metres)

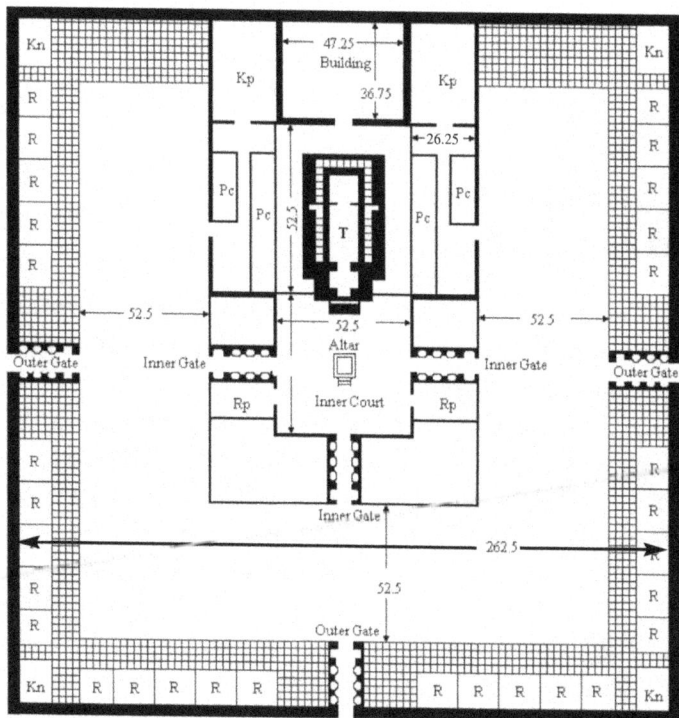

Key
Kn Kitchen for people's sacrifices.
Kp Priests' kitchens
Rp Rooms for ministering priests
Pc Chambers for priests
R   Rooms
T   Temple

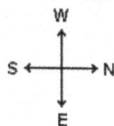

"The Millennial Temple" (used with permission) is based on the diagram found in *The Bible Knowledge Commentary, Old Testament*, (Victor Books, 1985), page 1303.

Chapter Five
My Beloved

"What [is] thy beloved more than [another] beloved, O thou fairest among women? what [is] thy beloved more than [another] beloved, that thou dost so charge us? My beloved [is] white and ruddy, the chiefest among ten thousand. His head [is as] the most fine gold, his locks [are] bushy, [and] black as a raven. His eyes [are] as [the eyes] of doves by the rivers of waters, washed with milk, [and] fitly set. His cheeks [are] as a bed of spices, [as] sweet flowers: his lips [like] lilies, dropping sweet smelling myrrh. His hands [are as] gold rings set with the beryl: his belly [is as] bright ivory overlaid [with] sapphires. His legs [are as] pillars of marble, set upon sockets of fine gold: his countenance [is] as Lebanon, excellent as the cedars. His mouth [is] most sweet: yea, he [is] altogether lovely. This [is] my beloved, and this [is] my friend, O daughters of Jerusalem." (Song 5:9-16)

The daughters of Jerusalem had been charged to tell the Beloved (should they find him first) that his bride was sick of love. In other words, she was so in love, it was making her ill. The daughters of Jerusalem ask, *"What is thy beloved more than another beloved, that thou dost so charge us?"* This reminds us of the pre-eminence of Christ as discussed in the last chapter and reminds us of the words of John the Baptist, *"He must increase, I [must] decrease"* (John 3:30). *"Behold, the Lamb of God which taketh away the sin of the world. This is he of whom I said, After me cometh a man which is preferred before me; for he was before me"* (John 1:29-30).

The bride goes on to give a delightful description of the one she loved. We shall consider it in fourteen parts ("My Beloved" having been dealt with previously):

1. White and ruddy;
2. The chiefest among ten thousand;
2. His head;
4. His locks;
5. His eyes;
6. His cheeks;
7. His lips;
8. His hands;
9. His belly;
10. His legs;
11. His countenance;
12. His mouth;
13. Altogether lovely; and,
14. My friend.

1. WHITE AND RUDDY

Remembering that Scripture interprets Scripture, we find that in Lamentations 4:7, *"Her Nazarites were purer than snow, they were whiter than milk, they were more ruddy in body than rubies, their polishing was of sapphire...".*

Therefore, there is a direct link between the Beloved and the Nazarite. The word Nazarite comes from the Hebrew meaning 'to separate' or 'to consecrate'. It identifies a person who has separated himself or herself to God under a special promise.

Consecration relates to a "filling of the hands". It is offering to God that which He has given us. In the case of the Nazarite, this was his/her life. In the circumstances of an ordinary vow, men consecrated some material possession, but the Nazarite consecrated himself or herself, and took a vow of separation. This related to some special service.

The Nazarite was specially raised up by God as an instrument of His power on behalf of His morally corrupt people when they were being attacked by enemies within their own borders. So Nazarites became numerous in Israel in periods of great religious or political excitement, and in Judges 5:2 we may paraphrase, "for the long-haired champions in Israel." They were raised up as a special token of God's favour to Israel. The tempting of them to break their vow by drinking wine was considered an aggravated sin (Amos 2:11-12). At the time of the captivity they were looked upon as a vanished glory in Israel (Lamentations 4:7 margin), but they reappeared in later history.

Numbers 6 outlines the principles governing the Nazarite. For example, there were the following prohibitions that have a spiritual meaning for us today:

A. HE MUST NOT TOUCH STRONG DRINK OR ANYTHING THAT CAME OF THE VINE

Proverbs 20:1 states: *"Wine [is] a mocker. Strong drink [is] raging: And whomsoever is deceived thereby is not wise."* In 31:4-5 we read: *"[It is] not for kings, O Lemuel, [it is] not for kings to drink wine; nor for princes strong drink; lest they drink and forget the law, and pervert the judgement of the afflicted.*" This is typical of turning away from things that may take control of us or distort our judgement. For example, we are exhorted not to be drunk with wine, but to be filled with the Spirit (Ephesians 5:18). When drunk with wine, we are out of control. When filled with the Spirit, every thing is in its correct perspective. Nevertheless, it is recommended for those about to perish (Proverbs 31:6) and can rejoice the heart of God and man when taken in moderation (Judges 9:13). So it can represent a temporary joy.

When we apply these principles to the Beloved, our Lord Jesus Christ, we remember that He is the Wisdom of God. He has loved righteousness and hated iniquity. He shall rule one day with a sceptre of righteousness. Psalm 72 predicts this day: *"Give the king thy judgements, O God, and thy righteousness unto the king's son. He shall judge thy people with righteousness, and thy poor with judgement…"* (verses 1-2). As for temporary joy, we know that Christ was the Man of Sorrows acquainted with grief while upon this earth. At the present time, He does not drink the fruit of the vine (see Luke 22:18). However, the day is quickly coming when He will see of the fruit of the travail of His soul and shall be satisfied. Then His kingdom shall be set up and there shall be an abundance of real joy. Just as Christ was separated to God, so are Christians. Christ said, *"For their sakes I sanctify myself, that they might be sanctified through the truth"* (John 17:19). So Christians share sorrowfully the rejection of their Lord. At the same time, they are encouraged to make judgements according to the truth that separates them to God.

B. No razor was to come upon the head of a Nazarite

This seems to represent a giving up of self and its rights in order that God's will is paramount and He is glorified. The Lord Jesus Christ could say, *"Nevertheless, not my will, but thine, be done"* (Luke 22:42) and *"I have glorified thee on the earth, I have finished the work which thou gavest me to do"* (John 17:4). It is imperative that Christians should renounce self and be all out for God the Father. Every good work is a selfless work done in the will of God for His glory. As Christians, we are new creatures in Christ expected to do good works (Ephesians 2:10): *"For we are his workmanship, created in Christ Jesus unto good works, which God hath before ordained that we should walk in them."*

To "create" or "found" is always an act of God as in "founding a city".

The place of our creation is in Christ Jesus – the ascended Messiah and Saviour. It is Christ who will be revealed by us. We are created for a purpose – to walk in good works. We are to walk as He walked – in love! (Ephesians 5:2).

So what are meant by "good works"? There are two words used for 'good' in the New Testament, namely, *agathos* and *kalos*. The word for 'work' is *ergon* that can mean 'deed' or 'business' also.

Agathos means good as a quality, whether physical or moral. For example:

Mark 10:18 (RV): "…Why callest thou me good? none is good save one…"

Matthew 5:45: evil ones and good ones

Matthew 7:11: "good gifts"

John 5:29: "…They that have done good…"

Romans 5:7: "good man".

It is also translated – kind, honourable or worthy. For example: *"Can any good thing come out of Nazareth?"* One who revealed God came from Nazareth. So "good" has the sense of reflecting God the most kind, honourable and worthy.

Kalos means beautiful, pleasing, noble or worthy in a moral sense.

Matthew 5:16: "…That they may see your good works…"

Matthew 26:10: "She hath wrought a good work upon me."

John 10:32: "Many good works have I shewed you…"

1 Timothy 5:4: "good and acceptable before God"

2 Timothy 4:7: the good fight

Titus 2:7: "good works"

Hebrews 6:5: "the good word of God"

From the above, we can define "Good Works" as being: unselfish and honourable acts completed in such a way that others receive the benefit and God receives the praise.

An example of such a work was the healing of the cripple – He went walking and leaping and praising God,

Acts 3:1-8: *"Now Peter and John went up together into the temple at the hour of prayer, [being] the ninth [hour]. And a certain man lame from his mother's womb was carried, whom they laid daily at the gate of the temple which is called Beautiful, to ask alms of them that entered into the temple; who seeing Peter and John about to go into the temple asked an alms. And Peter, fastening his eyes upon him with John, said, Look on us. And he gave heed unto them, expecting to receive something of them. Then Peter said, Silver and gold have I none; but such as I have give I thee: in the name of Jesus Christ of Nazareth rise up and walk. And he took him by the right hand, and lifted [him] up: and immediately his feet and ankle bones received strength. And he leaping up stood, and walked, and entered with them into the temple, walking, and leaping, and praising God."*

The works of Christ are described as "good" in John 10:32: *"Jesus answered them, Many good works have I shewed you from my Father; for which of those works do ye stone me?"*

Those works are listed in Luke 4:18: *"The Spirit of the Lord [is] upon me, because he hath anointed me to preach the gospel to the poor; he hath sent me to heal the broken-hearted, to preach deliverance to the captives, and recovering of sight to the blind, to set at liberty them that are bruised, to preach the acceptable year of the Lord."*

The works of the disciples are also supposed to be "good": *"Let your light so shine before men, that they may see your good works, and glorify your Father which is in heaven"* (Matthew 5:16).

We find the kind of good works to be done by the disciples of Christ in the Lord's fast in Isaiah 58:6-12: *"[Is] not this the fast that I have chosen? to loose the bands of wickedness, to undo the heavy burdens, and to let the oppressed go free, and that ye break every yoke? [Is it] not to deal thy bread to the hungry, and that thou bring the poor that are cast out to thy house? when thou seest the naked, that thou cover him; and that thou hide not thyself from thine own flesh?*

Then shall thy light break forth as the morning, and thine health shall spring forth speedily: and thy righteousness shall go before thee; the glory of the LORD shall be thy rereward. Then shalt thou call, and the LORD shall answer; thou shalt cry, and he shall say, Here I [am]. If thou take away from the midst of thee the yoke, the putting forth of the finger, and speaking vanity; and [if] thou draw out thy soul to the hungry, and satisfy the afflicted soul; then shall thy light rise in obscurity, and thy darkness [be] as the noonday: and the LORD shall guide thee continually, and satisfy thy soul in drought, and make fat thy bones: and thou shalt be like a watered garden, and like a spring of water, whose waters fail not. And [they that shall be] of thee shall build the old waste places: thou shalt raise up the foundations of many generations; and thou shalt be called, The repairer of the breach, The restorer of paths to dwell in."

There are, of course, many good works that pass unseen having been privately accomplished: *"Likewise also the good works [of some] are manifest beforehand; and they that are otherwise cannot be hid"* (1 Timothy 5:25).

The works of Dorcas were good: *"Now there was at Joppa a certain disciple named Tabitha* (gazelle), *which by interpretation is called Dorcas: this woman was full of good works and almsdeeds which she did"* (Acts 9:36).

The kind and power of her good works are seen in the response to her death: *"Then Peter arose and went with them.*

When he was come, they brought him into the upper chamber: and all the widows stood by him weeping, and shewing the coats and garments which Dorcas made, while she was with them" (Acts 9:39). Such works are appreciated by God. There is a group of Christian residents in an old people's home in Ipswich who have knitted many a hat for sailors. These were distributed by a port missionary lending "love" to his work.

In 1 Timothy 2:10, men's prayer and women's clothing are marks of godliness with good works. In 1 Timothy 5:10 a widow is well reported of for good works if she had:

- brought up children,
- lodged strangers,
- washed the saints' feet,
- relieved the afflicted, and
- diligently followed every good work.

Families of widows (1 Timothy 5:4) are also able to perform good works: *"But if any widow have children or nephews, let them learn first to shew piety at home, and to requite their parents: for that is good and acceptable before God."*

We may then consider good works in relation to government and law. In Romans 13:3 we read: *"For rulers are not a terror to good works, but to the evil. Wilt thou then not be afraid of the power? do that which is good, and thou shalt have praise of the same."*

Therefore, if we:

- obey the God-given authority then we are doing good;
- refuse to do that which is unrighteous, we are also doing good.

In 1 Timothy 6:18 we find a wealth. The believers are classed as rich in good works. They accumulate in their God-given nature the desire to do good. They are a treasure chest of good works.

Two of the good works are listed:

- ready to distribute – to be prepared to give generously! The widow in Mark 12:42 is an example of this.

- willing to communicate – to happily share equally among the saints! The Philippian Christians are an example of this (Philippians 4:14).

In the Second Epistle to Timothy, we can see how we can responsibly prepare ourselves unto good works. *"If a man therefore purge himself from these, he shall be a vessel unto honour, sanctified, and meet for the master's use, [and] prepared unto every good work"* (2 Timothy 2:21).

This is **preparation by Separation** from those whose teaching is so false that it overthrows faith. From such unrighteousness, we have to depart. There is much of this kind of teaching in the established church today. We are not to partake of their sins. We are not called upon to try to put them right. We are called to depart from them to gather with those faithful to the Lord. If we do this, then 2 Timothy 3:17 refers to us: *"That the man of God may be perfect, throughly **furnished** unto all good works."*

Preparation by Imitation is found in 2 Timothy 3:14, 17: *"Continue thou in the things which thou hast learned and hast been assured of, knowing of whom thou hast learned [them]."* The man of God is fully prepared to meet every circumstance with good works.

Preparation through Inspiration is found in 2 Timothy 3:16 where God's Word is available for teaching, reproof, correction and a guide to righteousness.

In Titus 2:7, we find that Christians should be a pattern of good works: *"In all things shewing thyself a **pattern** of good works: in doctrine [shewing] uncorruptness, gravity, sincerity...".* Here the word for 'pattern' means 'an impression, the mark of a blow'. So the moral power of leadership is to be an example of good works.

In Titus 2:14 Christians are encouraged to be zealous of good works: *"Who gave himself for us, that he might redeem us from all iniquity, and purify unto himself a peculiar people, **zealous** of good works."* In this verse, "zealous" means "uncompromising". It has the idea of having an earnest commitment to good works.

In Titus 3:8, we find an exhortation to give careful consideration to presiding or ruling over good works. That is to say, there is a sense of consciously being in control of good works so that they do not flag. *"[This is] a faithful saying, and these things I will that thou affirm constantly, that they which have believed in God might be careful to maintain good works. These things are good and profitable unto men."*

The result is fruit for God. Titus 3:14 – *"And let ours also learn to maintain good works for necessary uses, that they be not unfruitful."*

Christians are also called upon to stimulate unto love and good works: *"And let us consider one another to provoke unto love and to good works"* (Hebrews 10:24).

Finally, in 1 Peter 2:12 we find that living an honest life glorifies God: *"Having your conversation honest among the Gentiles: that, whereas they speak against you as evildoers, they may by [your] good works, which they shall behold, glorify God in the day of visitation."*

C. THE NAZARITE MUST NOT TOUCH A DEAD BODY

The wages of sin being death, the dead body would represent sin and its judgement. So the believer is to keep from all appearance of evil. He must not involve himself in that which would defile him. Christ is the Holy One. As stated previously, He knew no sin. He did no sin. In fact, there was no sin in Him. It is important to note that He could not sin!

The Nazarite was a vessel of power used by God to deliver His people from suffering under the hands of their enemies (e.g. Samson) or to make preparation for events to come (e.g. John the Baptist). The Father sent the Son to be the Saviour of the world. He was clearly set apart for this mission. Jesus said, *"Say ye of him, whom the Father hath sanctified, and sent into the world, thou blasphemest; because I said, I am the Son of God?"* (John 10:36). He, the true Nazarite, was sanctified and sent by the Father. Praise both Father and Son for the greatness of their love!

When the period of separation was complete, the ceremonial of release had to be gone through. It consisted of the presentation of burnt, sin and peace offerings with their accompaniments as detailed in Numbers 6:13-21, the shaving of the head and the burning of the hair of the head of separation, after which the Nazarite returned to ordinary life.

If we look briefly at the word "ruddy", then we find it is used to describe David in 1 Samuel 16:12, *"...Now he [was] ruddy, [and] withal of a beautiful countence, and goodly to look to."* David was obviously a handsome youth, but beauty is in the eye of the beholder. God could see that David was a man after His own heart. That was his true beauty. So it is with the Lord Jesus Christ. He is the man after God's own heart – *"This is my beloved Son, in whom I am well pleased"* (Matthew 3:17).

Of course, the Nazarite was "as ruddy *in body* as rubies". We remember the body of our Lord Jesus Christ when we celebrate the Lord's Supper. He said of the bread: "This is my body which is given for you…" The bread of the Supper is a photograph of Christ to our souls. It was a body prepared for Him so that He could experience death. It was His own body in which He bore our sins on the tree (1 Peter 2:24). It is through the offering of His body that Christians are sanctified (Hebrews 10:10). In Colossians 1:21-22, we read: *"And you, that were sometime alienated and enemies in [your] mind by wicked works, yet now hath he **reconciled** in the body of his flesh through death, to present you holy and unblameable and unreproveable in his sight."*

Yet, His body was described as a temple of the Holy Spirit (John 2:21). In fact, the fullness of the Godhead resides in Him bodily (Colossians 2:9). No doubt, it still is – but as a "glorious body" (Philippians 3:21). It is in this body that we shall see Him in a future day. It is in this glorious body that Zion will view their Messiah when He appears to deliver them from their enemies.

2. The Chiefest among Ten Thousand

According to Strong, *dagal*, the Hebrew word for 'chiefest', comes from a primitive root 'to flaunt', i.e. 'raise a flag'. Figuratively, it means "to be conspicuous". Hence, the use of "chiefest". According to Young's concordance, it has the force of 'standard-bearer'. So, the beloved is called "the chiefest" or "standard-bearer" (AV margin).

A. THE STANDARD-BEARER

In Numbers chapter 2, we find that the children of Israel pitched their camps by their standard (*degel*) and each family by its own ensign (*oth*). In Isaiah 59:19 we read, *"When the enemy shall come in like a flood, the Spirit of the LORD shall lift up a standard against him."* So when there is opposition to the people of God, then the Holy Spirit raises a banner in their defence. This shows that the one with the standard has responsibility to protect the people it represents. So the people gathered to the standard and, of course, to their standard-bearer.

Genesis 49:10 states, *"The sceptre shall not depart from Judah, nor a lawgiver from between his feet, until Shiloh come; and unto him [shall] the gathering of the people [be]."* Shiloh is a name given to the Messiah as the "Prince of Peace". In a day to come, the people will gather to Him.

Of that royal tribe, Judah, Nahshon the son of Amminadab was the captain or "lifted up" one. His name means 'oracle', the speaking place of God. There is only One who has revealed God in a full way and that is Christ Himself. He has manifested and declared the Father. He is the Word who was with God, and who is God. He is the very expression of the nature and will of God – the brightness of God's glory and the express image of His person. He is the Alpha and Omega, the beginning and the end, the first and the last (Revelation 22:13). As Alpha and

Omega, He is the One who has given a full revelation of God and His purposes. As the beginning and the end, He is the Source, Sustainer and Completer of creation. As the First and the Last, He is the LORD (Yahweh), the ever-existent One. The latter reminds us of Exodus 17:15: *"And Moses built an altar, and called the name of it Jehovah-nissi."* The name *Jehovah-nissi* means 'the Lord our banner'.

Of course, the name the First and the Last is particular important in regard to Israel. The First and the Last is identified as Jesus in Revelation 22: *"I am Alpha and Omega, the beginning and the end, the first and the last"* (verse 13). The speaker is revealed a few verses afterwards: *"I, Jesus, have sent mine angel to testify unto you these things in the churches. I am the root and the offspring of David, [and] the bright and morning star"* (verse 16). As the Alpha and Omega, Jesus is the full revelation of God, His will, counsels and His purposes. He is the One whom we should hear: *"Hearken unto me, O Jacob and Israel, my called; I [am] he; I [am] the first, I also [am] the last"* (Isaiah 48:12). The apostle John received the book of Revelation directly from the Alpha and Omega: *"I am Alpha and Omega, the first and the last: and, What thou seest, write in a book, and send [it] unto the seven churches which are in Asia; unto Ephesus, and unto Smyrna, and unto Pergamos, and unto Thyatira, and unto Sardis, and unto Philadelphia, and unto Laodicea"* (Revelation 1:11).

As the Beginning and the Ending, He is the Creator and Sustainer of everything. In Isaiah 48:13, the First and the Last goes on to say: *"Mine hand also hath laid the foundation of the earth, and my right hand hath spanned the heavens."* While in Isaiah 41:4, the same Person states: *"Who hath wrought and done [it], calling the generations from the beginning? I the LORD, the first, and with the last;*

I [am] he." The "*I am he*" emphasises that He is the same. The unchanging One.

The name the First and the Last emphasises that He is God. This is clearly seen from Isaiah 44:6: "*Thus saith the LORD the King of Israel, and his redeemer the LORD of hosts; I [am] the first, and I [am] the last; and beside me there [is] no God.*" This must have been especially comforting to the apostle John in Revelation 1:17: "*And when I saw him, I fell at his feet as dead. And he laid his right hand upon me, saying unto me, Fear not; I am the first and the last.*" No need to fear even though in the very presence of God.

It is of interest that the book of Revelation not only deals with the church age, but goes on to describe in detail the time of Jacob's Trouble – the Great Tribulation. It tells of two returns of the Jews to Israel and ends with the new Jerusalem.

Of course, Christ is the captain of our salvation (Hebrews 2:10) – the author and finisher of faith (Hebrews 12:2). His banner over us is love and it is our joy to be gathered to His name. The Lord Jesus Christ stated that where two or three are gathered together in His name, He would be in the midst of them. It is, therefore, a wonderful privilege to meet with fellow believers in the presence of the Son of God Himself. This may be when we come together for prayer, for the Lord's Supper or under the teaching of God's servants. Think of it; the Lord is there! Oh that we might apprehend and advertise the thought more and our churches would be filled with joy and praise.

Furthermore, speaking of Christ, Isaiah writes, "*And in that day there shall be a root of Jesse, which shall stand for an ensign of the people; to it shall the Gentiles seek: and his rest shall be glorious*" (Isaiah 11:10).

B. THE PRE-EMINENT ONE

Young's Literal Translation of the Holy Bible translates the verse as, *"My beloved is clear and ruddy, Conspicuous above a myriad!"* This shows that He is the greatest! Whether as prophet, priest or king, there is none to compare with Him. Typically, it speaks of Christ as the One highest in dignity and rank – the Pre-eminent One!

Romans 8:29 reveals that Christ, as man, is the highest in rank within the family of God: *"For whom he did fore-know, he also did predestinate [to be] conformed to the image of his Son, that he might be the firstborn among many brethren."*

Colossians 1:15 shows that He is the One who is far above any other in creation because He is the Creator and Sustainer of all things. *"Who is the image of the invisible God, the firstborn of every creature".* By Him all things consist. All things were made on account of Him – for His pleasure.

Colossians 1:18 tells us that regarding resurrection, He, The Son of the Father's love, is the chief: *"And he is the head of the body, the church: who is the beginning, the first-born from the dead; that in all [things] he might have the preeminence."* Revelation 1:5 informs us that of all those resurrected, Jesus Christ has the first place. How the Father delights to honour the Son!

Hebrews 1:6 ensures that the Son is seen as God's first-born. *"And again, when he bringeth in the firstbegotten into the world, he saith, And let all the angels of God worship him."* He is the pre-existent One whom God loves and honours in a unique way. The One God brought into the world through manhood. The subject of angelic worship.

The Firstborn

O God, Thou hast now spoken –
In Son Thy word we see;
The Centre of creation;
The perfect stamp of Thee.
In joyful resurrection,
His glory shall appear –
The Christ above all others
That from the grave shall rear.

O Lord, Thou hast appointed
Saints fashioned like Thy Son
That, He, Thy blest Anointed
Should be the greatest One.
His brethren shall surround Him,
Those for whom He bled;
Their crowns they'll cast before Him
Their own most loving Head.

O God, Thou hast commanded
Angels to worship One
In Whom Thy heart delighteth
Thine own most precious Son.
Into the world Thou'lt bring Him
In glory and great pow'r;
The Earth shall cease her groaning
And righteousness shall flow'r.

(G. E. Stevens, 2004)

3. HIS HEAD

"His head [is as] the most fine gold." (Song 5:11)

The answer to the scriptural symbolism of a head of gold is found in Daniel 2:36-38: *"This [is] the dream; and we will tell the interpretation thereof before the king. Thou, O king, [art] a king of kings: for the God of heaven hath given thee a kingdom, power, and strength, and glory. And where-*

soever the children of men dwell, the beasts of the field and the fowls of the heaven hath he given into thine hand, and hath made thee ruler over them all. Thou [art] this head of gold."

In these verses, Nebuchadnezzar is identified as being a king of kings. His kingdom was given to him by God along with all his power, strength and glory. But, the Beloved in the Song of Songs has a head of *most* fine or, better, pure gold. Some would say the "gold of gold". It therefore speaks of the King of kings and Lord of lords. He is the King of that kingdom Daniel states is set up by the God of heaven – a kingdom that will never be destroyed. It stands for ever (Daniel 2:44).

This is probably a pertinent place to consider the dream of Nebuchadnezzar and its interpretation because it contains a major prophecy concerning what Christ called the "Times of the Gentiles" (Luke 21:24): *"And they shall fall by the edge of the sword, and shall be led away captive into all nations: and Jerusalem shall be trodden down of the Gentiles, until the times of the Gentiles be fulfilled."* The prophetic dream then goes on to speak of the coming kingdom. We read of the whole kingdom in Daniel 2:25-49:

"Then Arioch brought in Daniel before the king in haste and said thus unto him, I have found a man of the captives of Judah, that will make known unto the king the interpretation. The king answered and said to Daniel, whose name [was] Belteshazzar, Art thou able to make known unto me the dream which I have seen, and the interpretation thereof? Daniel answered in the presence of the king, and said, The secret which the king hath demanded cannot the wise [men], the astrologers, the magicians, the soothsayers, shew unto the king; but there is a God in heaven that revealeth secrets, and

maketh known to the king Nebuchadnezzar what shall be in the latter days.

Thy dream, and the visions of thy head upon thy bed, are these; as for thee, O king, thy thoughts came [into thy mind] upon thy bed, what should come to pass hereafter: and he that revealeth secrets maketh known to thee what shall come to pass. But as for me, this secret is not revealed to me for [any] wisdom that I have more than any living, but for [their] sakes that shall make known the interpretation to the king, and that thou mightest know the thoughts of thy heart.

DIAGRAM 3: NEBUCHADNEZZAR'S DREAMED IMAGE

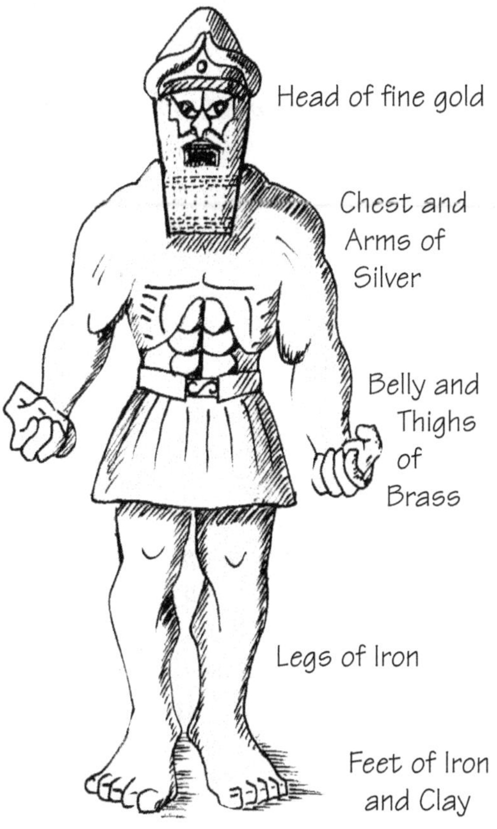

Thou, O king, sawest, and behold a great image. This great image, whose brightness [was] excellent, stood before thee; and the form thereof [was] terrible. This image's head [was] of fine gold, his breast and his arms of silver, his belly and his thighs of brass, his legs of iron, his feet

Head of fine gold

Chest and Arms of Silver

Belly and Thighs of Brass

Legs of Iron

Feet of Iron and Clay

103

*part of iron and part of clay. Thou sawest till that a stone was
cut out without hands, which smote the image upon his feet
[that were] of iron and clay, and brake them to pieces. Then
was the iron, the clay, the brass, the silver, and the gold, broken to pieces together, and became like the chaff of the
summer threshingfloors; and the wind carried them away,
that no place was found for them: and the stone that smote
the image became a great mountain, and filled the whole
earth.*

*This [is] the dream; and we will tell the interpretation thereof
before the king. Thou, O king, [art] a king of kings: for the
God of heaven hath given thee a kingdom, power, and
strength, and glory. And wheresoever the children of men
dwell, the beasts of the field and the fowls of the heaven hath
he given into thine hand, and hath made thee ruler over
them all. Thou [art] this head of gold. And after thee shall
arise another kingdom inferior to thee, and another third
kingdom of brass, which shall bear rule over all the earth.
And the fourth kingdom shall be strong as iron: forasmuch as
iron breaketh in pieces and subdueth all [things]: and as iron
that breaketh all these, shall it break in pieces and bruise.
And whereas thou sawest the feet and toes, part of potters' clay,
and part of iron, the kingdom shall be divided; but there
shall be in it of the strength of the iron, forasmuch as thou
sawest the iron mixed with miry clay. And as the toes of the
feet [were] part of iron, and part of clay, [so] the kingdom
shall be partly strong, and partly broken. And whereas thou
sawest iron mixed with miry clay, they shall mingle themselves with the seed of men: but they shall not cleave one to
another, even as iron is not mixed with clay. And in the days
of these kings shall the God of heaven set up a kingdom,
which shall never be destroyed: and the kingdom shall not be
left to other people, [but] it shall break in pieces and consume
all these kingdoms, and it shall stand for ever. Forasmuch as*

thou sawest that the stone was cut out of the mountain without hands, and that it brake in pieces the iron, the brass, the clay, the silver, and the gold; the great God hath made known to the king what shall come to pass hereafter: and the dream [is] certain, and the interpretation thereof sure.

Then the king Nebuchadnezzar fell upon his face, and worshipped Daniel, and commanded that they should offer an oblation and sweet odours unto him. The king answered unto Daniel, and said, Of a truth [it is], that your God [is] a God of gods, and a Lord of kings, and a revealer of secrets, seeing thou couldst reveal this secret. Then the king made Daniel a great man, and gave him many great gifts, and made him ruler over the whole province of Babylon, and chief of the governors over all the wise [men] of Babylon. Then Daniel requested of the king, and he set Shadrach, Meshach, and Abed-nego, over the affairs of the province of Babylon: but Daniel [sat] in the gate of the king."

Elsewhere in the book of Daniel it is made clear as to which kingdoms these metals and parts represented (Table 1). However, we do well to notice that, as we descend from the head of the image, the kingdoms that are represented become more inferior.

Returning to the subject of pure gold, we find that it also speaks of **holiness**. In Exodus 39: 30, we find the plate of pure gold that the high priest wore upon his mitre. Engraved upon it were the words, "Holiness to the Lord". In the book of Revelation, we find the *holy* city of pure gold. It is God who sits upon the throne of His holiness. It is the Lord who is to be worshipped in the beauty of holiness.

Therefore, the purest gold symbolises **Deity**. The King who reigns shall be God. *"For unto us a child is born, unto us a son is given: and the government shall be upon his*

TABLE 1:

THE KINGDOMS OF THE GENTILES UP TO THE MILLENNIAL KINGDOM OF CHRIST

The Parts of Nebuchadnezzar's Image (Daniel 2)	The Beasts (Daniel 7)	The Kingdoms Represented	Approximate Time they Commenced
Head of fine gold – Daniel 2:32	The lion – Daniel 7:4	Babylonian	606 BC
Breast and arms of silver – Daniel 2:32	The bear – Daniel 7:5 The ram – Daniel 8:3, 20-21	Medo-Persian	538 BC
Belly and thighs of brass – Daniel 2:32	The leopard – Daniel 7:6 The goat – Daniel 8:5, 20-21	Grecian	336 BC
Legs of iron – Daniel 2:33	The great and terrible beast – Daniel 7:7	Roman – Revelation 13	30 BC
Feet part iron and part clay – Daniel 2:33 & 41-43	Part of previous	Democratic Roman	AD 364
Stone cut (without hands) out of the mountain – Daniel 2:35 & 44-45	None mentioned but may be represented by the Lion of the tribe of Judah.	Millennial – Daniel 7:14, 27; Revelation 20:4	Future

Note: Today, we are living under the Democratic Roman period. Although Israel is no longer under Gentile rule (becoming a nation again in 1948), the nation is under a democratic rule and remains without a king. Yet the battle for Jerusalem continues.

*shoulder: and his name shall be Wonderful, Counsellor, **The Mighty God**, The Everlasting Father and The Prince of Peace. Of the increase of [his] government and peace [there shall be] no end"* (Isaiah 9:6-7). He will order and establish the kingdom. He will sit upon the throne of David.

These five names of Jesus are awe-inspiring! The number "five" symbolising how the grace of God has met the failed responsibility of man.

Christ is **Wonderful** because of His:

- Person – God become man – John 1, Philippians 2, 1 Timothy 3:16.

- Name – *"Unto you is born this day in the city of David a Saviour, which is Christ the Lord"* (Luke 2:11).

- Love – *"And walk in love, as Christ also hath loved us, and hath given himself for us an offering and a sacrifice to God for a sweetsmelling savour"* (Ephesians 5:2).

- Worth – John 8.46: *"Which of you convinceth me of sin?"* 2 Chronicles 2:9: *"Even to prepare me timber in abundance: for the house which I am about to build [shall be] wonderful great"* (Compare John 2:19-21).

- Works – Psalm 111:4: *"He hath made his wonderful works to be remembered: the LORD [is] gracious and full of compassion."* Matthew 21:15: *"And when the chief priests and scribes saw the wonderful things that he did, and the children crying in the temple, and saying, Hosanna to the Son of David; they were sore displeased."*

- Words – Luke 4.22: *"And all bear him witness, and wondered at the gracious words which proceeded out of his mouth."*

- Witness – Psalm 119:129: *"Thy testimonies [are] wonderful: therefore doth my soul keep them."*

- Will – Luke 22:42: *"Nevertheless, not my will..."* Hebrews 10:7: *"Lo, I come to do thy will..."*

Christ is **Counsellor** because of His:

- Omniscience – Isaiah 28:29: *"This also cometh forth from the LORD of hosts, [which] is wonderful in counsel, [and] excellent in working."* Numbers 27:21: *"And he shall stand before Eleazar the priest, who shall ask [counsel] for him after the judgement of Urim before the LORD: at his word shall they go out, and at his word they shall come in, [both] he, and all the children of Israel with him, even all the congregation."* Christ revealed His omniscience in the case of "seeing" Nathanael beforehand in John 1:48 and in the knowledge of a fish to be caught by Peter that had a coin in its mouth (Matthew 17:27).

- Wisdom – Proverbs 8:14: *"Counsel [is] mine, and sound wisdom: I [am] understanding; I have strength."* Christ is called the Wisdom of God (1 Corinthians 1:24).

- Teacher – Isaiah 40:13: *"Who hath directed the Spirit of the LORD, or [being] his counsellor hath taught him?"* Christ taught with authority (Mark 1:22).

- Truth – Isaiah 25:1: *"O LORD, thou [art] my God; I will exalt thee, I will praise thy name; for thou hast done wonderful [things]; [thy] counsels of old [are] faithfulness [and] truth."* Grace and truth came by Jesus Christ (John 1:17).

- Guidance – Judges 18:5: *"And they said unto him, Ask counsel, we pray thee, of God, that we may know whether our way which we go shall be prosperous."*

Peter knew that the Christ had the words of eternal life (John 6:68).

- Being King and Priest – Zechariah 6:13: *"Even he shall build the temple of the Lord; and he shall bear the glory, and shall sit and rule upon his throne; and he shall be a priest upon his throne: and the counsel of peace shall be between them both."* Christ is an high priest after the order of Melchizedek – king and priest.

- Being the Subject of God's Counsel – Acts 2:23: *"Him, being delivered by the determinate counsel and foreknowledge of God, ye have taken, and by wicked hands have crucified and slain:"*

- Being Judge – Revelation 3:18: *"I counsel thee to buy of me gold tried in the fire, that thou mayest be rich; and white raiment, that thou mayest be clothed, and [that] the shame of thy nakedness do not appear; and anoint thine eyes with eyesalve, that thou mayest see."*

He is the **The Mighty God** who is all powerful (omnipotent). He is:

- The Lord of Hosts – Jeremiah 32:18: *"Thou shewest lovingkindness unto thousands, and recompensest the iniquity of the fathers into the bosom of their children after them: the Great, the Mighty God, the LORD of hosts, [is] his name…"*

- Yahweh – Psalm 50:1: *"A Psalm of Asaph. The mighty God, [even] the LORD, hath spoken, and called the earth from the rising of the sun unto the going down thereof."*

- The Mighty God of Jacob – Psalm 132:2: *"How he sware unto the LORD, [and] vowed unto the mighty [God] of Jacob…"*

- Shiloh – Isaiah 10:21: *"The remnant shall return, [even] the remnant of Jacob, unto the mighty God."*

Jesus claimed to be God by saying that:

- all should honour the Son just as they honour the Father (John 5:23);

- He and His Father are one (John 10:30);

- He who has seen Him has seen the Father (John 14:9);

- Before Abraham was, He was (I am – John 8:58).

Christ is the **Everlasting Father** – The Source of Eternity. This shows us that He is the eternal and unchanging (immutable) source of all. Verses that indicate this are:

- Isaiah 63:16: *"Doubtless thou [art] our father, though Abraham be ignorant of us, and Israel acknowledge us not: thou, O LORD, [art] our father, our redeemer; thy name [is] from everlasting."*

- Micah 5:2: *"But thou, Bethlehem Ephratah, [though] thou be little among the thousands of Judah, yet out of thee shall he come forth unto me [that is] to be ruler in Israel; whose goings forth [have been] from of old, from everlasting."*

- Psalm 90:2: *"Before the mountains were brought forth, or ever thou hadst formed the earth and the world, even from everlasting to everlasting, thou [art] God."*

- Psalm 93:2: *"Thy throne [is] established of old: thou [art] from everlasting."*

- John 3:16: *"For God so loved the world, that he gave his only begotten Son, that whosoever believeth in him should not perish, but have everlasting life."*

- John 3:36: *"He that believeth on the Son hath everlasting life: and he that believeth not the Son shall not see life; but the wrath of God abideth on him."*
- John 6:40: *"And this is the will of him that sent me, that every one which seeth the Son, and believeth on him, may have everlasting life: and I will raise him up at the last day."*
- John 6:47: *"Verily, verily, I say unto you, He that believeth on me hath everlasting life."*

He is also the **Prince of Peace**.

In the reign of Christ over this earth the mountains shall bring peace to the people (Psalm 72:3). The reason for this being that mercy and truth are met together and righteousness and peace have kissed each other (Psalm 85:8, 10). Where or when did this happen? At the cross, the place of the skull. There the Lord Jesus made peace through the blood of his cross. Today, Christians can echo the words of Paul: *"Therefore being justified by faith, we have peace with God through our Lord Jesus Christ"* (Romans 5:1). They have been reconciled to God. There is no enmity and no fear of judgement for sin. The price has been paid.

On account of this, the peace of God can rule in their hearts. That is to say, no matter what the trials or circumstances, Christians have the assurance that God is for them – always working for their ultimate blessing. Jesus was emphasising this to His disciples prior to the cross when He said, *"Peace I leave with you, my peace I give unto you: not as the world giveth, give I unto you. Let not your heart be troubled, neither let it be afraid"* (John 14:27).

Peace for His disciples was a principle desire of the Lord Jesus. His presence with them was introduced by peace:

"And as they thus spake, Jesus himself stood in the midst of them, and saith unto them, Peace [be] unto you" (Luke 24:36).

"Then the same day at evening, being the first [day] of the week, when the doors were shut where the disciples were assembled for fear of the Jews, came Jesus and stood in the midst, and saith unto them, Peace [be] unto you. ... Then said Jesus to them again, Peace [be] unto you: as [my] Father hath sent me, even so send I you. ...

And after eight days again his disciples were within, and Thomas with them: [then] came Jesus, the doors being shut, and stood in the midst, and said, Peace [be] unto you" (John 20:19, 21, 26).

The words He spoke to His disciples were to promote peace in their hearts despite trials: *"These things I have spoken unto you, that in me ye might have peace. In the world ye shall have tribulation: but be of good cheer; I have overcome the world"* (John 16:33).

In Ephesians we find Christ is our peace: *"For he is our peace, who hath made both one, and hath broken down the middle wall of partition [between us]"* (Ephesians 2:14). The "us" in this verse refers to Jew and Gentile. Through faith in Him there is no longer a barrier between us because we share the same Christ.

Yet, think of the Lord Jesus as He wept over Jerusalem. He said, *"If thou hadst known, even thou, at least in this thy day, the things [which belong] unto thy peace! but now they are hid from thine eyes"* (Luke 19:42). Had they received Him, then the kingdom would have been set up and Jerusalem would have become true to her name – *Possessor of Peace.*

The promise of peace to Zion is found in Isaiah 66:12: *"For thus saith the LORD, Behold, I will extend peace to her like a river, and the glory of the Gentiles like a flowing stream: then shall ye suck, ye shall be borne upon [her] sides, and be dandled upon [her] knees."*

This peace would be lasting: *"For the mountains shall depart, and the hills be removed; but my kindness shall not depart from thee, neither shall the covenant of my peace be removed, saith the LORD that hath mercy on thee. ... And all thy children [shall be] taught of the LORD; and great [shall be] the peace of thy children"* (Isaiah 54: 10, 13).

What joy there will be in Jerusalem: *"How beautiful upon the mountains are the feet of him that bringeth good tidings, that publisheth peace; that bringeth good tidings of good, that publisheth salvation; that saith unto Zion, Thy God reigneth!"* (Isaiah 52:7).

God had promised this peace to the house of David: *"But upon David, and upon his seed, and upon his house, and upon his throne, shall there be peace for ever from the LORD"* (1 Kings 2:33). This will be fulfilled through Christ: *"In his days shall the righteous flourish; and abundance of peace so long as the moon endureth"* (Psalm 72:7).

God will make a covenant of peace with Israel: *"Moreover I will make a covenant of peace with them; it shall be an everlasting covenant with them: and I will place them, and multiply them, and will set my sanctuary in the midst of them for evermore"* (Ezekiel 37:26).

In Isaiah we read: *"And the work of righteousness shall be peace; and the effect of righteousness quietness and assurance for ever"* (Isaiah 32:17). The springboard of peace is righteousness. Both are found in Christ as a priest for ever after the order of Melchizedek for He is King of righteousness and King of peace (Hebrews 7). In 2 Thessalonians, we find the "Lord of peace" who Himself gives peace (2 Thessalonians 3:16).

We are also very conscious that peace is part of the fruit of the Spirit. It should mark Christians who, through Christ, know the God of peace. For this reason Christians are encouraged to endeavour to keep the unity of the Spirit in the bond of peace (Ephesians 4). The unity of the Spirit cannot be broken, but the bond of peace can.

As we consider these names of the Lord Jesus, we recognise that He is greater than Solomon! His glory will shade that of Solomon's into insignificance. He said that the glory of Solomon could not be compared to the glory of the lily of the field. But the Son of God is the Creator. His glory must, therefore, surpass that of the lily.

Furthermore, as Creator, He is able to bring peace to nature itself: *"And he arose, and rebuked the wind, and said unto the sea, Peace, be still. And the wind ceased, and there was a great calm"* (Mark 4:39).

In Isaiah 53:5 we see the relationship between the Prince of Peace and suffering:

"But he [was] wounded for our transgressions, [he was] bruised for our iniquities: the chastisement of our peace [was] upon him; and with his stripes we are healed."

In the following scriptures we see the relationship between the Prince of Peace and illness:

Mark 5:34: *"And he said unto her, Daughter, thy faith hath made thee whole; go in peace, and be whole of thy plague."*

Luke 8:48: *"And he said unto her, Daughter, be of good comfort: thy faith hath made thee whole; go in peace."*

Furthermore, there is the relationship of the Prince of Peace and sin:

Luke 7:50: *"And he said to the woman, Thy faith hath saved thee; go in peace."*

Christ has made peace by the blood of His cross. The faith of this sinful woman brings her under the anticipated sacrifice of Christ. Hence, He can tell her to go in peace. The Prince of Peace had to suffer if we were to be reconciled to God. We are healed from sin through His offering as our Substitute – Isaiah 53:5: *"... With his stripes we are healed."*

Acts 10:36 focuses on Christ as the agent of peace: *"The word which [God] sent unto the children of Israel, preaching peace by Jesus Christ: (he is Lord of all)."*

It is in the Son that it pleases the Father that all fulness should dwell (Colossians 1:19). All the fulness of Deity is found in the Son. It is in Christ that all the fulness of the Godhead dwells bodily (Colossians 2:9).

Essentially, He is:

- Omnipresent – all present (John 3:13; Matthew 18:20; 28:19-20);

- Omnipotent – all powerful (John 6:35; 14:11; 10:25-38; 15:24);

- Omniscient – all knowing (John 2:24-25; 18:4);

- Immutable – unchanging (Hebrews 1:12; 13:8);

- Self-existent (John 8:58; 1:4; 5:26); and,

- Eternal (Revelation 1:8; John 3:16 and 5:26).

His moral attributes include:

- Holiness (Mark 1:24; Revelation 4:8);

- Righteousness (1 Corinthians 1:30; Jeremiah 23:5-6; 1 John 2:1-2);

- Love (1 John 4:16-19);

- Faithfulness (John 14:6; 1 John 5:20).

It may be as well to consider the "head" of the Lord Jesus Christ while He was here on earth. For example, in Matthew 8:20 we read that Jesus said, *"The foxes have holes, and the birds of the air [have] nests; but the Son of man hath not where to lay [his] head."* The title "The Son of man" speaks of Christ as the Man who has full authority in earth and heaven. It seems to embrace the fact that He is the Son of David (royalty) and the Son of Abraham (promise).

It is through the seed of Abraham that all the nations of the earth are blessed. It is through the seed of David that a king shall reign in righteousness. How great He is and yet He was a homeless stranger in the world His hands had made. Generally speaking, there was no home for Him to live in during His years of ministry. He came to bless His own people, but they did not receive Him.

Linked with this, we read in Matthew 21:42 that Jesus is the Stone that the builders rejected. He was the unrecognised Stone and Shepherd of Israel (Genesis 49:24). However, Matthew 21:42 continues, *"The stone which the builders rejected, the same is become the head of the corner: this is the Lord's doing, and it is marvellous in our eyes?"*

1 Peter 2 reminds us that Jesus is the chief corner stone laid in Zion. He is "elect" (chosen) and "precious" (held in honour) – verse 6. In verse 7, He is the stone rejected by the builders. In verse 4, He is described as the living stone. So Christ is the One from whom the edifice of the church takes her lines.

Elect and Precious

O Christ, elect and precious,
Of God – the Anointed One,
We hail Thee who hast loved us,
The Chief and Corner Stone!

We praise Thee as our Saviour,
As God's Beloved Son
Who by Thy grace hath bought us
And for us glory won.

O Christ, elect and precious,
Prophet of God through birth,
Mighty in word and action –
Jesus of Nazareth!
The Holy One of Israel,
The God of the whole earth!
We bow to Thee in worship,
And so declare Thy worth.

O Christ, elect and precious,
King David's promised Seed,
Sent here by God the Father
To meet our ruined need!
The Sign in depth and height,
In virgin's womb conceived;
Thy name's Immanuel –
The mighty God indeed!

O Christ, elect and precious,
Thou for Thy church hast died:
The pearl of such great value,
The everlasting bride!
She thought on her Beloved,
And vanquishing her pride,
"Thou'rt altogether lovely!
And Wonderful!" she cried.

(G. E. Stevens, 1988)

Matthew 27:29-37 tells us of soldiers who had no appreciation of His Person, and we see His head was crowned and His body was smitten: *"And when they had platted a crown of thorns, they put [it] upon his head, and a reed in his right hand: and they bowed the knee before him, and mocked him, saying, Hail, King of the Jews! And they spit upon him, and took the reed, and smote him on the head. ...And set up over his head his accusation written, THIS IS JESUS THE KING OF THE JEWS."* The Lord Jesus could have wiped them out with a sigh, but He had the Father's will to accomplish.

In contrast, we find a worshipper in Mary who fully appreciated that He was the Son of God, *"And being in Bethany in the house of Simon the leper, as he sat at meat, there came a woman having an alabaster box of ointment of spikenard very precious; and she brake the box, and poured [it] on his head"* (Mark 14:3). It was not unusual for women of that day to keep such ointment for the day of their wedding. Here, in devoted worship, Mary anoints the head of Jesus with the costly oil.

In John 20:7-12 we see that which had covered His head is an emblem of His resurrection. *"And the napkin, that was about his head, not lying with the linen clothes, but wrapped together in a place by itself. ... And seeth two angels in white sitting, the one at the head, and the other at the feet, where the body of Jesus had lain."*

When considering headship, Paul writes in 1 Corinthians 11:3-10: *"But I would have you know, that the head of every man is Christ; and the head of the woman [is] the man; and the head of Christ [is] God. Every man praying or prophesying, having [his] head covered, dishonoureth his head. But every woman that prayeth or prophesieth with [her] head uncovered dishonoureth her head: for that is even all one as if she were shaven. ... For a man indeed ought not to cover [his] head, forasmuch as he is the image and glory of God: but the woman is the glory of the man. ... For this cause ought the woman to have power on [her] head because of the angels."* This gives the order of authority and responsibility in the sight of God – God, Christ, man and then woman. Christ submits to the will of God. The man submits to the will of Christ and therefore to God. The woman submits to the man, Christ and God.

In Ephesians 1:22 we read, *"And hath put all [things] under his feet, and gave him [to be] the head over all [things] to the church."* God has put all things under the power of Christ. He is pre-eminent in power. Therefore, He has this power to control all things relating to the church. This will be seen at His appearing, when the church shall be seen sharing in His glory.

Ephesians 5:25 explains that Christ is the Head of the church for which He gave Himself in love. It should be easy to submit to the One who still loves us in such great measure, because we know He has our good at heart at all times.

In Colossians 1:18 *"...He is the head of the body, the church: who is the beginning, the firstborn from the dead; that in all [things] he might have the preeminence."* As Head of the body, Christ is the Life-giver, Sustainer and Controller. As the "Beginning" we see Him as the Source of Origin. As the "Firstborn from among the dead" we see that He is the proven Son of God and that His resurrection was not only foreordained, but also His personal right because His life was sinless.

Colossians 2:10 takes the headship of Christ further: *"And ye are complete in him, which is the head of all principality and power."* Here Christ has sovereign rights over all other forms of rule or rulers whether angels or otherwise. All should submit to Him. *"And not holding the Head, from which all the body by joints and bands having nourishment ministered, and knit together, increaseth with the increase of God"* (verse 19). It is also through the nourishment (supply) that comes from the Head that the body of Christ is knit together (united) and grows.

Revelation 14:14 describes His head as crowned, but He is acting in judgement; in chapter 19 His head is crowned with many crowns showing both the vast scope of His offices as priest and king, but also the fact that He is worthy!!!

The Headship of Christ

The fulness of the times draws near,
Purposed by God and clearly read,
When things in earth and things in heav'n
Be gathered in the Christ, their Head.
United in that wondrous day
They all bow to His righteous sway.

It must be told, it must be known,
The Head of Christ is God, pure love!
Bowed to His will while Man below –
A Servant still in heaven above.
Let us submit to Him in turn;
From His example may we learn.

Christ of the body, Saviour He,
The Head of the purchased church, His bride.
How matchless is our Bridegroom's love
Measured in that He bled and died.
Always may He our first love be –
He is altogether lovely!

(G. E. Stevens, 2002)

4. His Locks

"His locks [are] bushy, [and] black as a raven." (Song 5:11)

Again, we can see the link with the Nazarite in the locks being bushy or flowing (Numbers 6:5). In the latter, it is a symbol of separation to God (sanctification). The person separated is to live a holy life. *"Be ye holy, for I am holy."* 2 Timothy 2:20-25 shows us the kind of lives Christians should live as those who are sanctified: *"But in a great house there are not only vessels of gold and of silver, but also of wood and of earth; and some to honour, and some to dishonour. If a man therefore purge himself from these, he shall be a vessel unto honour, sanctified, and meet for the master's use, [and] prepared unto every good work. Flee also youthful lusts: but follow righteousness, faith, charity, peace, with them that call on the Lord out of a pure heart. But foolish and unlearned questions avoid, knowing that they do gender strifes. And the servant of the Lord must not strive; but be gentle unto all [men], apt to teach, patient, in meekness instructing those that oppose themselves; … ".* Christ the Shepherd King will certainly be fit for the Master's use. As a man here, He was characterised by righteousness, faith, love and peace. His heart was pure.

It is more difficult to see from other scriptures why the beloved's hair is described "as black as a raven" because the bird was an unclean one, and the word "black" usually refers to the result of famine or some kind of departure from the Lord. However, if we consider the hair of Christ as Judge seen in Revelation 1:14, we find that its whiteness speaks of purity and wisdom. Christ is the "Wisdom of God". In Daniel's visions in chapter seven of his book, the Ancient of Days has hair like this. So, whiteness refers to age and wisdom. Black, flowing hair would indicate youth and vitality.

Proverbs 20 tells us that *"the glory of young men [is] their strength: and the beauty of old men [is] the gray head"* (verse 29). It seems that Revelation 1:18 answers to the flowing, black hair: *"I [am] he that liveth, and was dead; and, behold, I am alive for evermore, Amen; and have the keys of hell and of death."* We have a Lord and Saviour who lives after the power of an endless life. He is the One who remains when all else has gone. He is the Same. *"And, Thou, Lord, in the beginning hast laid the foundation of the earth; and the heavens are the works of thine hands: they shall perish; but thou remainest; and they all shall wax old as doth a garment; and as a vesture shalt thou fold them up, and they shall be changed: but thou art the same, and thy years shall not fail"* (Hebrews 1:10-12). Praise God!

5. HIS EYES

"His eyes [are] as [the eyes] of doves by the rivers of waters, washed with milk, [and] fitly set." (Song 5:12)

A. EYES

In Isaiah 6:5 we read, *"Then said I, Woe [is] me! for I am undone; because I [am] a man of unclean lips, and I dwell in the midst of a people of unclean lips: for mine eyes have seen the King, the LORD of hosts."* This verse identifies the antitype of the beloved of the Song of Songs. He is the visible king and Lord of hosts. When we compare this verse with John 12, we see that the person whose glory was seen by Isaiah was none other than that of the Lord Jesus Christ. He is both God and the King. Therefore, if we apply these thoughts to other scriptures relating to the "eyes", we find: *"The eyes of the LORD [are] in every place, beholding the evil and the good. A king that sitteth in the throne of judgement scattereth away all evil with his eyes"* (Proverbs 15:3; 20:8).

As the Lord, He sees everything – everywhere! This is encouraging and challenging to the behaviour of Christians, but must be quite unsettling to unbelievers. This is taken further in Hebrews 4:13, *"Neither is there any creature that is not manifest in his sight: but all things [are] naked and opened unto the eyes of him with whom we have to do."* This verse would challenge our thoughts and motives, besides our actions.

It is not surprising then, that the King scatters away all evil with His eyes. As Revelation 1:14 reveals, the eyes of the Lord Jesus are as a flame of fire. They are discerning and consuming. This is supported by Habakkuk 1:13, *"[Thou art] of purer eyes than to behold evil, and canst not look on iniquity…".*

However, the thought in the Song of Songs is that His eyes are for us. *"If God [be] for us, who [can be] against us?"* (Romans 8:31). As our great high priest, the Lord Jesus sympathises with us and supports us. 1 Peter 3:12 reads, *"For the eyes of the Lord [are] over the righteous, and his ears [are open] unto their prayers: but the face of the Lord [is] against them that do evil."* He is watching over us in order to protect and, if necessary, correct us. He also hears our prayers – that is to say, He will answer our prayers according to His will and with our blessing at heart.

This is confirmed by Psalm 34:15, *"The eyes of the LORD [are] upon the righteous, and his ears [are open] unto their cry."* Furthermore, 2 Chronicles 16:9 says, *"For the eyes of the LORD run to and fro throughout the whole earth, to shew himself strong in the behalf of [them] whose heart [is] perfect toward him."* Here we find the Lord extremely active on our behalf. He is the One who stands between us and our enemies – our Defender. The ranging of His eyes throughout the whole earth shows His constancy – and He does not slumber or sleep. What a Protector! What a Provider!

In Zechariah 4:10 we find seven lamps that run to and fro throughout the earth. In Revelation 5:6 we find that they are the seven eyes or seven Spirits of God sent forth into the whole earth (compare Isaiah 11:1-3). We find a similar thought in Psalm 33:18, *"Behold, the eye of the LORD [is] upon them that fear him, upon them that hope in his mercy."* His eyes are merciful.

Also, Psalm 32:8 tells us that the eyes of the Lord guide us, *"I will instruct thee and teach thee in the way which thou shalt go: I will guide thee with mine eye."* In Proverbs 22:12, His eyes suggest omniscience: *"The eyes of the LORD preserve knowledge, and he overthroweth the words of the transgressor."*

Israel knows that the Lord is ultimately for them because Isaiah expresses this hope: *"Thine eyes shall see the king in his beauty: they shall behold the land that is very far off"* (Isaiah 33:17); and Deuteronomy 11:12 says, *"A land which the LORD thy God careth for: the eyes of the LORD thy God [are] always upon it, from the beginning of the year even unto the end of the year."* Israel's inheritance is secure.

B. AS THE EYES OF DOVES

This may be literally translated *"His eyes as doves..."* (YLT). This is supported by J. N. Darby's New Translation, *"His eyes are like doves..."* (Song 5:12, N.Tr.). So the simile supports the meaning that the eyes were like "doves" – not like "doves' eyes". There may be several reasons for comparing them in this way because doves are:

a. Beautiful birds – *"Though ye have lien among the pots, [yet shall ye be as] the wings of a dove covered with silver, and her feathers with yellow gold"* (Psalm 68:13) and, *"O my dove, [that art] in the clefts of the rock, in the secret [places] of the stairs, let me see thy countenance, let me hear thy voice; for sweet [is] thy voice, and thy countenance [is] comely"* (Song 2:14).

b. Faithful to their mates – *"...Mourn sore like doves"* (Isaiah 59:11);

c. Harmless – *"Behold, ... harmless as doves"* (Matthew 10:16);

d. Pure – *"My dove, my undefiled is [but] one..."* (Song 6:9).

We can apply these facets of the dove to Christ. His beauty may be seen in the silver and the gold, the former speaking of the glory of redemption and reflecting His love unto death for us – even when we were enemies of God. The latter speaks of the glory of divine righteousness. Job could say, *"[When] he hath tried me, I shall come forth as gold"* (Job 23:10). The action of trial under the hand of the Lord God results in cleansing in the case of Job. The Lord Jesus Christ was tried in all points, yet without sin. There was no sin in Him. His righteousness was divine. Nonetheless, He learned obedience through suffering. That is to say, He learned the cost of obedience in the physical sense. He was obedient unto death – even the death of the cross! As Son before incarnation, He knew what it was to speak and it was done. Yet as the Son before the Father, He also knew how to obey: *"Here am I; send me"* (Isaiah 6:8). Therefore, the link between His sufferings as a man and obedience seems to reflect the cost of doing the Father's will. The climax of His obedience being the death of the cross where He was to be accursed of God.

The whiteness of the dove relates directly to purity. In Daniel 12:10 we find, *"Many shall be made purified, and made white, and tried…"*. Christ, Himself, was undefiled. He knew no sin. He did no sin. There was no sin in Him. In His priesthood, it is written of Him, *"For such an high priest became us, [who is] holy, harmless, undefiled, separate from sinners, and made higher than the heavens"* (Hebrews 7:26).

Interestingly, the word 'harmless' is also used in the scripture relating to Christ as high priest. It means 'guileless' – that is, without cunning or deceit. It is a mark of open honesty. 1 Peter 2:22-23 states, *"…Who did no sin, neither was guile found in his mouth, who, when he was reviled, reviled not again; when he suffered, he threatened not; but committed [himself] to him that judgeth righteously."*

It is understood that the dove keeps the same mate throughout its life. When the partner dies, then the dove mourns. This expresses the faithfulness of Christ to His bride. This is seen in the preparation that He makes for His church in Ephesians 5:25-27: *"Husbands, love your wives, even as Christ also loved the church, and gave himself for it; that he might sanctify and cleanse it with the washing of water by the word, that he might present it to himself a glorious church, not having spot, or wrinkle, or any such thing; but that it should be holy and without blemish."*

Furthermore, the dove reminds us of the qualities of the Holy Spirit. In Luke 3:22 we read, *"And the Holy Ghost descended in a bodily shape like a dove upon him, and a voice came from heaven, which said, Thou art my beloved Son; in thee I am well pleased."*

C. BY THE RIVERS OF WATERS

The poetry suggests the glistening of clear eyes and indicates that these water-brooks are life-giving and fruitful. In Isaiah 32:2 we find a man who is as rivers of water in a dry land. This is the Messiah, the King. Hence, Proverbs 21:1 applies, *"The king's heart [is] in the hand of the LORD, [as] the rivers of water: he turneth it whithersoever he will"*. Precious thought, the heart of the King desires life and growth in His people under the controlling hand of God. *"Blessed [is] the man that walketh not in the counsel of the ungodly, nor standeth in the way of sinners, nor sitteth in the seat of the scornful. But his delight [is] in the law of the LORD; and in his law doth he meditate day and night. And he shall be like a tree planted by the rivers of water, that bringeth forth his fruit in his season; his leaf also shall not wither; and whatsoever he doeth shall prosper"* (Psalm 1:1-3). Christ Himself is the perfect example of this kind of man.

D. WASHED WITH MILK

The eyes are bathed in milk. Milk is known for its whiteness (Lamentations 4:7). This has been discussed above. However, in Isaiah 66:11, we find that milk also represents the consolations and abundant glory that come through Jerusalem when the LORD extends peace to her like a river. So the Prince of Peace, the Mighty God, will both comfort and delight His bride.

In Leviticus 20:24 we find that the promised land was one flowing with milk and honey. In other words, it was a land of abundant blessing. So the eyes of the Lord promise an abundance of blessing for His people.

However, in Hebrews 5:12 we find that milk is indicative of the first principles of the oracles of God. Therefore, the eyes of Christ being washed with milk are those that have been purified by the word of God.

E. AND FITLY SET

The eyes are said to "sit" or "abide" in fulness. It would seem that this filling relates to the aspects found in the following passage: *"And this I pray, that your love may abound yet more and more in knowledge and [in] all judgement; that ye may approve things that are excellent; that ye may be sincere and without offence till the day of Christ; being filled with the fruits of righteousness, which are by Jesus Christ, unto the glory and praise of God"* (Philippians 1:9-11).

The "fruits of righteousness" are transferred to us from the One who Himself is filled with them – along with abounding love, the approval of things excellent before God and, the desire to glorify and praise Him.

6. HIS CHEEKS

"His cheeks [are] as a bed of spices, [as] sweet flowers..." (Song 5:13)

In order to gain a picture of the meaning of these similes, we will consider:

    a.   the cheeks of the beloved;

    b.   the bed of spices; and,

    c.   the sweet flowers.

A. CHEEKS

When we consider Christ as the Man of Sorrows, acquainted with grief, we remember the prophetic scriptures that speak of His cheek/s:

- Job 16:10 expresses the feelings of Job which parallel those of Christ in years to come: *"They have gaped upon me with their mouth; they have smitten me upon the cheek reproachfully; they have gathered themselves together against me."*

- Micah 5:1 shows that there would be a total disrespect for dignified Christ: *"Gather thyself in troops, O daughter of troops: he hath laid siege against us: they shall smite the judge of Israel with a rod upon the cheek."*

- Isaiah 50:6 reveals how Christ would submit Himself to physical sufferings for righteousness' sake: *"I gave my back to the smiters, and my cheeks to them that plucked off the hair: I hid not my face from shame and spitting."*

Throughout these scriptures, the beating and striking of the cheek is linked with reproach. Therefore, the cheeks would represent the opposite when dressed with spices. They speak of honour and worth. *"And they sung a new song, saying, Thou art worthy to take the book, and to open the seals thereof: for thou wast slain, and hast redeemed us to God by thy blood out of every kindred, and tongue, and people, and nation; and hast made us unto our God kings and priests: and we shall reign on the earth"* (Revelation 5:9-10).

B. BED OF SPICES

The bed of spices reminds us that our Beloved, the Lord Jesus Christ, is a present (gift of God), a preserver and precious.

The first reference to spices in the Bible is Genesis 43:11: *"And their father Israel said unto them, If [it must be] so now, do this; take of the best fruits in the land in your vessels, and carry down the man a present, a little balm, and a little honey, spices, and myrrh, nuts, and almonds…"*

In 1 Kings 10:10 we find the queen of Sheba including spices in her gift to King Solomon: *"And she gave the king an hundred and twenty talents of gold, and of spices very great store, and precious stones: there came no more such abundance of spices as these which the queen of Sheba gave to king Solomon."* These verses show that spices were used as valuable gifts. When we apply this to Christ, we see that He is precious! He is God's unspeakable gift. There are no words to describe Him fully. He is a gift that expresses the love of God towards men: *"For God so loved the world that he gave his only begotten Son…"* (John 3:16).

2 Kings 20:13 emphasises the preciousness of spices: *"And Hezekiah hearkened unto them, and shewed them all the house of his precious things, the silver, and the gold, and the spices, and the precious ointment, and [all] the house of his armour, and all that was found in his treasures: there was nothing in his house, nor in all his dominion, that Hezekiah shewed them not."* 1 Peter 2:7 (RV) states that Christ is "preciousness" to those who believe.

In Exodus 25:6, we discover that spices were used in the holy anointing oil during the time of the tabernacle system. Exodus 30:23-24 identifies the spices used, *"Take thou also unto thee principal spices, of pure myrrh five hundred [shekels], and of sweet cinnamon half so much, [even] two hundred and fifty [shekels], and of sweet calamus two hundred and fifty [shekels], and of cassia five hundred [shekels]."* Under our previous discussions on "myrrh" we concluded that olive oil spoke of the Spirit of the LORD;

cassia spoke of the spirit of wisdom and understanding; calamus and cinnamon the spirit of counsel and might; and, pure myrrh the spirit of knowledge and the fear of the LORD. All are found in perfection in Christ. The reasons for His anointing are given in Luke 4:18-19: *"The Spirit of the Lord [is] upon me, because he hath anointed me to preach the gospel to the poor; he hath sent me to heal the brokenhearted, to preach deliverance to the captives, and recovering of sight to the blind, to set at liberty them that are bruised, to preach the acceptable year of the Lord."*

In 2 Chronicles 16:14 we find that spices were used when burying the dead: *"And they buried him in his own sepulchres, which he had made for himself in the city of David, and laid him in the bed which was filled with sweet odours and divers kinds [of spices] prepared by the apothecaries' art: and they made a very great burning for him."* This is one of the main uses in New Testament times (compare Mark 16:1; Luke 23:56; 24:1). It would seem that spices were used within the linen wrapping to act as a preservative. It reminds us that Jesus is our Saviour, Deliverer and Keeper.

C. SWEET FLOWERS

This has been translated by J.N. Darby as, *"raised beds of sweet plants"*. Young translates it "towers of perfumes". We know from Proverbs 18:10 that the name of the Lord is a strong tower. He is our Defender! This gives us the assurance that God is for us.

The garments of the anointed king in Psalm 45:8 smell of myrrh and aloes and cassia. This is a Messianic Psalm. It depicts the time when Christ will ride prosperously in His majesty because of truth, meekness and righteousness. He shall be a warrior king whose arrows are sharp in the heart of His enemies. The result is that His people praise Him for ever and ever. Yet, He greatly desires the beauty of His queen (in that day, Zion). She shall dwell safely in His palace. How much more the Lord is active for our defence today and He has prepared a place for His heavenly bride, the church, in the Father's house on high.

7. HIS LIPS

"His lips [like] lilies dropping sweet smelling myrrh." (Song 5:13)

In this section of our study, we will consider the meanings of:

    a. lips;

    b. lilies; and,

    c. sweet smelling myrrh.

A. LIPS

When we consider the lips of the Lord Jesus, we move quickly to Psalm 45:2: *"Thou art fairer than the children of men: grace is poured into thy lips: therefore God hath blessed thee for ever."* Grace is the favour of God manward. It has been called "love in action". The apostle John records that the Word (who was ever face to face with God, yet God Himself) became flesh and dwelt among us full of grace and truth (John 1:14). A few verses later, he states that grace and truth came by Jesus Christ (verse 17).

The apostle Paul records: *"For ye know the grace of our Lord Jesus Christ, that, though he was rich, yet for your sakes he became poor, that ye through his poverty might be made rich"* (2 Corinthians 8:9). He gave up His *possessions* when He came into this world. He was so poor during His public ministry that He had to ask for a coin on one occasion. But the idea of the *poverty* of Christ would also show that when he had nothing more to give, He gave Himself. It is pertinent to note the acrostic of GRACE here, namely, God's Redemption At Christ's Expense. The purpose for

His downstooping love was that we might be blessed with forgiveness, eternal life and all other benefits of redemption.

Yet Psalm 45 emphasises that this grace is poured into His lips. In the lips of the King was grace stored. It flowed out in His ministry here and the people wondered at the gracious words that proceeded out of His mouth (Luke 4:22).

As to the Lord Jesus Christ as the King, Proverbs 16:10, 21 apply: *"A divine sentence [is] in the lips of the king: his mouth transgresseth not in judgement. ... The wise in heart shall be called prudent: and the sweetness of the lips increaseth learning."* These verses remind us that the judgement of Christ is always a righteous judgement and, furthermore, being the Wisdom of God, His lips contain the knowledge that increases learning. Mary knew this. She sat at His feet and listened to His teaching. Proverbs 20:15 says, *"There is gold, and a multitude of rubies: but the lips of knowledge [are] a precious jewel."* Mary sat at the feet of the One who was omniscient – He knew all things. We can do the same. What a privilege!

In his life's experience, Job was able to say, *"Neither have I gone back from the commandment of his lips; I have esteemed the words of his mouth more than my necessary [food]"* (Job 23:12). This reminds us of the Lord Jesus who told us that man should not live by bread alone, but by every word that proceeds from the mouth of God (Matthew 4:4). Furthermore, Proverbs 10:21 states: *"The lips of the righteous feed many: but fools die for want of wisdom."* The words that the Lord Jesus spoke were the words of His Father. They promoted spiritual growth. Also, as He was righteous in all His ways, then He was able to give guidance: *"The lips of the righteous know what is acceptable: but the mouth of the wicked [speaketh] frowardness"* (Proverbs 10:32).

We see the Lord Jesus leading the praises in the church (Hebrews 2:12). This readily fits in with the encouragement for our lips to praise in Hebrews 13:15: *"By him therefore let us offer the sacrifice of praise to God continually, that is, the fruit of [our] lips giving thanks to his name."*

Lips may also be used for preaching. Psalm 40:9 reads, *"I have preached righteousness in the great congregation: lo, I have not refrained my lips, O LORD, thou knowest."* The Lord Jesus preached (Matthew 4:4). We are also to preach (Colossians 1:28).

B. LILIES

Lilies are recognised for their growth and their beauty or glory. They also teach us dependence upon God. Hosea 14:5 reads, *"I will be as the dew unto Israel: he shall grow as the lily, and cast forth his roots as Lebanon."* This reminds us of the words at the end of Luke 2: *"And Jesus increased in wisdom and stature, and in favour with God and man."* This covers all the important areas of life. "Wisdom" shows learning and its application. "Stature" reveals physical growth. "Favour with God" indicates spiritual growth and obedience. "Favour with man" emphasises social development and relationships. May we be good stewards and seek to increase in the same ways! All too often, we neglect the social aspect by separating ourselves to the point of isolation. Very often, we find that we neglect our physical appearance and fitness.

If Hosea pinpoints the growth of the lily, Jesus, in Luke 12:27, identifies its dependence and beauty: *"Consider the lilies how they grow: they toil not, they spin not; and yet I say unto you, that Solomon in all his glory was not arrayed like one of these."* The Lord Jesus Himself was the dependent Man (Psalm 16). He relied completely upon God. He did the Father's will. He was obedient unto death – even the death of the cross. It is a lesson that we must learn. The lily is, of course, beautiful in its appearance. Its beauty reflects the glory of its Creator. So the lips of our Lord Jesus brought glory to God. May ours bring glory to His name also!

C. SWEET-SMELLING MYRRH

Myrrh is so-called from its bitterness. Nonetheless, its fragrance is undeniably pleasant. It therefore speaks of the sufferings of Christ (bitterness) and the blessing (fragrance) relating to the perfection of those sufferings. This is seen in the following scripture: *"And walk in love, as Christ also hath loved us, and hath given himself for us an offering and a sacrifice to God for a sweet smelling savour"* (Ephesians 5:2).

If this is the measure of the love of Christ, then our lives should follow the same course of self-denial so that we might be a sweet savour of Christ unto God (2 Corinthians 2:15). One way in which this may be expressed is through giving. In Philippians 4:18 Paul expresses his gratitude for the Philippians' gift: *"But I have all, and abound: I am full, having received of Epaphroditus the things [which were sent] from you, an odour of a sweet smell, a sacrifice acceptable, well pleasing to God."* May our lives be a sweet fragrance to God as we follow in the steps of our Master and give sacrificially in love.

8. HIS HANDS

"His hands [are as] gold rings set with the beryl..."
(Song 5:14)

There are many references to "hands" in the Bible. They are mainly concerned with work (Mark 6:2), fellowship (Acts 6:6), prayer (1 Timothy 2:8) and blessing (Luke 24:50).

A. WORK

In relation to the Son of God, we read in Mark 6:2, *"And when the sabbath day was come, he began to teach in the synagogue: and many hearing him were astonished, saying, From whence hath this man these things? and what wisdom is this which is given unto him, that even such mighty works are wrought by his hands?"* In John 17:4, we find, *"I have glorified thee on the earth; I have finished the work which thou gavest me to do."* These words He could pray to His Father in anticipation of that final cry from the cross, *"It is finished!"* (John 19:30). All was completed as far as divine purpose for mankind was concerned.

B. FELLOWSHIP

Galatians 2:9 gives us a passage linking hands to fellowship: *"And when James, Cephas, and John, who seemed to be pillars, perceived the grace that was given unto me, they gave to me and Barnabas the right hands of fellowship; that we [should go] unto the heathen, and they unto the circumcision."*

The fellowship that existed between the Son and His Father was expressed in the Lord's own words in John 10:30, *"I and [my] Father are one."* In 1 John 1:3 we find that the fellowship of the apostles was with the Father, and with His Son Jesus Christ. So the fellowship in the Godhead moves towards believers. 1 Corinthians 1:9 tells us, *"God [is] faithful, by whom ye were called unto the fellowship of his Son Jesus Christ our Lord."* This speaks of the Son of God uniting us to Himself. It leads to fellowship with one another: *"If we say that we have fellowship with him, and walk in darkness, we lie, and do not the truth: but if we walk in the light, as he is in the light, we have fellowship one with another, and the blood of Jesus Christ his Son cleanseth us from all sin"* (1 John 1:6-7).

In Acts 2:42 the early Christians *"continued stedfastly in the apostles' doctrine and fellowship, and in breaking of bread, and in prayers."* May God give us the grace to do the same. Yet they went further. At the end of the chapter which is so often neglected, we read: *"And all that believed were together, and had all things common; and sold their possessions and goods, and parted them to all [men], as every man had need"* (verses 44-45). Here we see love in action. It is love for one another that is the mark of true discipleship. There is no greater witness to unbelievers.

C. PRAYER

In 1 Timothy 2:8 Paul exhorts the men to lift up holy hands and pray. We know that the Lord Jesus, as a dependent Man, prayed. In Matthew 14:23 we find Him alone on the mountain, praying – the privacy of prayer! Luke 6:12 shows us an occasion where He spent all night in prayer to God – the measure of His dependence! John 17 reveals the intimacy and detail of one of His prayers. In verses 1-5, He expresses His desires for Himself that the Father may be glorified in Him. From verses 6-19, He expresses the position of His disciples and asks the Father to keep them so that He is glorified in them. Finally, He prays for all who believe as a result of the disciples' witness and desires that they will be glorified with Him (verses 20-26).

In Hebrews 5:7 we find the fervency of His prayers in Gethsemane (the place of the oil press) revealed: *"Who in the days of his flesh, when he had offered up prayers and supplications with strong crying and tears unto him that was able to save him from death..."* Apply this knowledge to His words found in Matthew 26 to understand the full impact of His suffering: *"And he went a little further, and fell on his face, and prayed, saying, O my Father, if it be possible, let this cup pass from me: nevertheless not as I will, but as thou[wilt]. And he cometh unto the disciples, and findeth them asleep, and saith unto Peter, What, could ye not watch with me one hour? Watch and pray, that ye enter not into temptation: the spirit indeed [is] willing, but the flesh [is] weak. He went away again the second time, and prayed, saying, O my Father, if this cup may not pass away from me, except I drink it, thy will be done"* (verses 39-42).

D. BLESSING

When we turn to Luke 24.50, we find that Jesus has led His disciples out to Bethany (the house of figs) where He lifted up His hands and blessed them. While He blessed them, He was parted from them and carried up into heaven. As a Man, he was carried into the very presence of God. Mark 16:19 tells us that He sat on the right hand of God – the place of favour and power. Peter records: *"He is gone into heaven, and is on the right hand of God: angels and authorities and powers being made subject to Him"* (1 Peter 3:22). Blessed assurance, all His power is active for us in blessing!

The following is a useful outline on the subject of "The Hands of Christ". It forms an acrostic of CHRIST.

Creating Hands: Hebrews 1:10.

Healing Hands: Mark 5:23; 6:5; 8:23.

Receiving Hands: Matthew 19:13; Mark 10:16.

Identifying Hands: Luke 24:39; John 20:20.

Supporting Hands: Luke 24:50.

Trusted Hands: John 13:3.

Creating Hands

Here are references to our Lord Jesus as the Creator:

Hebrews 1:10-12: *"And, Thou, Lord, in the beginning hast laid the foundation of the earth; and the heavens are the works of thine hands…"*

Isaiah 45:12, 18: *"I have made the earth, and created man upon it: I, [even] my hands, have stretched out the heavens, and all their host have I commanded. … For thus saith the LORD that created the heavens; God himself that formed the earth and made it; he hath established it, he created it not in vain, he formed it to be inhabited: I [am] the LORD; and [there is] none else."*

Healing Hands

Below, we can see why the Lord Jesus is called the Great Physician by many:

Mark 5:23: *"And besought him greatly, saying, My little daughter lieth at the point of death: [I pray thee,] come and lay thy hands on her, that she may be healed; and she shall live."*

Mark 6:5: *"And he could there do no mighty work, save that he laid his hands upon a few sick folk, and healed [them]."*

Mark 8:23, 25: *"And he took the blind man by the hand, and led him out of the town; and when he had spit on his eyes, and put his hands upon him, he asked him if he saw ought. … After that he put [his] hands again upon his eyes, and made him look up: and he was restored, and saw every man clearly."*

Luke 13:11-13: *"And, behold, there was a woman which had a spirit of infirmity eighteen years, and was bowed together, and could in no wise lift up [herself]. And when Jesus saw her, he called [her to him], and said unto her, Woman, thou art loosed from thine infirmity. And he laid [his] hands on her: and immediately she was made straight, and glorified God."*

Receiving Hands

We see in the following verses how happily the Lord Jesus received children – but He will not turn away any who come to Him in faith.

Matthew 19:13-15: *"Then were there brought unto him little children, that he should put [his] hands on them, and pray: and the disciples rebuked them. ... And he laid [his] hands on them, and departed thence."*

Mark 10:16: *"And he took them up in his arms, put [his] hands upon them, and blessed them."*

Identifying Hands

The references that follow show how Christ identified Himself in resurrection to His disciples.

Luke 24:39-40: *"Behold my hands and my feet, that it is I myself: handle me, and see; for a spirit hath not flesh and bones, as ye see me have. And when he had thus spoken, he shewed them [his] hands and [his] feet."*

John 20:20-27: *"And when he had so said, he shewed unto them [his] hands and his side. Then were the disciples glad, when they saw the Lord. ... The other disciples therefore said unto him [Thomas], We have seen the Lord. But he said unto them, Except I shall see in his hands the print of the nails, and put my finger into the print of the nails, and thrust my hand into his side, I will not believe. ... Then saith he to Thomas, Reach hither thy finger, and behold my hands; and reach hither thy hand, and thrust [it] into my side: and be not faithless, but believing."*

It is worthy of note that this is the only scripture that refers to nails being the instruments by which the hands and feet of our Lord were pierced.

Supporting Hands

The scripture that follows shows how the priestly blessing and support of Christ was first made apparent. He is a blessing priest after the order of Melchizedek.

Luke 24:50: *"And he led them out as far as to Bethany, and he lifted up his hands, and blessed them."*

Trusted Hands

In John 13:3, Christ is trusted implicitly by His Father.

"Jesus knowing that the Father had given all things into his hands, and that he was come from God, and went to God..."

GOLD RINGS

We have already noted that gold speaks of the glory of Divine righteousness. This is seen in the perfect life of Christ; but why compare hands to "gold rings"? Gold rings are associated with acceptance, authority, sonship, faithful witness and secure judgement.

Acceptance and Authority

In Genesis 41:42-43 we find that Joseph is accepted and given a position of authority: *"And Pharaoh took off his ring from his hand, and put it upon Joseph's hand, and arrayed him in vestures of fine linen, and put a gold chain about his neck; and he made him to ride in the second char-*

iot which he had; and they cried before him, Bow the knee: and he made him [ruler] over all the land of Egypt." In the same way, Christ is set on the right hand of the majesty on high. He is both Prince and Saviour.

Esther 8:2, 8 emphasise the use of a ring as being a sign of acceptance and authority: "And the king took off his ring, which he had taken from Haman, and gave it unto Mordecai. And Esther set Mordecai over the house of Haman. ... Write ye also for the Jews, as it liketh you, in the king's name, and seal [it] with the king's ring: for the writing which is written in the king's name, and sealed with the king's ring, may no man reverse."

Sonship

Luke 15:22 shows us what happened to the prodigal son when he returned to his father. "The father said to his servants, Bring forth the best robe, and put [it] on him; and put a ring on his hand, and shoes on [his] feet..." The son was given back his position in his father's house. The robe speaks of righteousness or dignity; the shoes speak of him as a free man rather than a slave; and the ring speaks of authority within the house. Today Christ is a Son over His own house – whose house we are (Hebrews 3:6). In the day of the Shepherd King we read, "Yet have I set my king upon my holy hill of Zion. I will declare the decree: The LORD hath said unto me, Thou [art] my Son; this day have I begotten thee" (Psalm 2:6-7). In that coming day men are commanded to kiss the Son lest He be angry and they perish from the way. We do this today because we love Him!

Faithful Witness

Exodus 25:14 states: "And thou shalt put the staves into the rings by the sides of the ark, that the ark may be borne with them." Other furniture in the tabernacle had golden rings.

The reason was that they had to be carried. So the rings would speak of the means whereby God's service is carried out on earth. They speak of a faithful witness. Jesus Christ is called such in Revelation 1:5. Furthermore, in Hebrews 3:1-2 we read, *"Wherefore, holy brethren, partakers of the heavenly calling, consider the Apostle and High Priest of our profession, Christ Jesus; who was faithful to him that appointed him..."*

Secure Judgement

Finally, in Exodus 39:21 we read: *"And they did bind the breastplate by his rings unto the rings of the ephod with a lace of blue, that it might be above the curious girdle of the ephod, and that the breastplate might not be loosed from the ephod; as the LORD commanded Moses."*

He is the anchor that secures judgement (breastplate) to the priesthood (ephod). The lace of blue reminds us of the commandments of the Lord. Christ has fulfilled the Law of God. He is able to judge righteously. He will be both King and Priest upon His throne. He is a priest for ever after the order of Melchizedek – King of Righteousness and King of Peace.

Furthermore, the breastplate contained the Urim (lights) and Thummin (perfections) by which the priest was guided in the will of God. These seem to have been a number of stones, combinations of which could say, "No" or "Yes" or give no definite answer. 1 Samuel 30:7-8 give us an example of this: *"And David said to Abiathar the priest, Ahimelech's son, I pray thee, bring me hither the ephod. And Abiathar brought thither the ephod to David. And David inquired at the LORD, saying, Shall I pursue after this troop? shall I overtake them? And he answered him, Pursue: for thou shalt surely overtake [them], and without fail recover [all]."*

BERYL

The Hebrew word for beryl is *tarshish* which means 'to batter or subdue'. We recall the words of Psalm 110: *"The LORD said unto my Lord, Sit thou at my right hand, until I make thine enemies thy footstool."* Christ, the King, shall rule with a rod of iron!

In Matthew 22:41-46 the Lord Jesus asked, *"What think ye of Christ? whose son is he?"* The Pharisees answered, *"The son of David."* Jesus said, *"How then doth David in spirit call him Lord, saying, The LORD said unto my Lord, Sit thou on my right hand, till I make thine enemies thy footstool? If David then call him Lord, how is he his son?"*

They could not answer Him. Yet Christ was acknowledged by David to be his Lord (*Adon* – Master). It shows that Christ in pre existence is the Son of God. It also teaches that the Son of God was to become man – the seed of David. Jesus could say, *"I am the root and the off-spring of David, [and] the bright and morning star"* (Revelation 22:16). He is both the Source (root) and descendant (offspring) of David. He is that morning star that heralds the new day for Israel. Being distinct in His being and witness, He can be described as "bright".

Furthermore, in 1 Corinthians 15:24-28 we have a majestic passage: *"Then [cometh] the end, when he shall have delivered up the kingdom to God, even the Father; when he shall have put down all rule and all authority and power. For he must reign, till he hath put all enemies under his feet. The last enemy [that] shall be destroyed [is] death. For he hath put all things under his feet. But when he saith all things are put under [him, it is] manifest that he is excepted, which did put all things under him. And when all things shall be subdued unto him, then shall the Son also himself be subject unto him that put all things under him, that God may be all in all."*

At the end of His millennial reign, Christ will have dealt with every enemy. Those who stand against Him at the end of that thousand years will be destroyed by fire from heaven. The Son then hands the purged kingdom back to God the Father.

Thus, the prophetic scripture is fulfilled. In Hebrews 2:5-9 we find, *"For unto the angels hath he not put in subjection the world to come, whereof we speak. But one in a certain place testified, saying, What is man, that thou art mindful of him? or the son of man, that thou visitest him? Thou madest him a little lower than the angels; thou crownedst him with glory and honour, and didst set him over the works of thy hands: thou hast put all things in subjection under his feet. For in that he put all in subjection under him, he left nothing [that is] not put under him. But now we see not yet all things put under him. But we see Jesus, who was made a little lower than the angels for the suffering of death, crowned with glory and honour; that he by the grace of God should taste death for every man."*

It was given to Adam to have dominion over this world. In this respect, he was crowned with glory and honour. Adam failed. So Jesus, the second man, the Lord from out of heaven came into this scene. He was to taste death for every thing in order that creation might cease her groaning and blossom as the rose. Isaiah 35 describes this beautifully: *"The wilderness and the solitary place shall be glad for them; and the desert shall rejoice, and blossom as the rose. It shall blossom abundantly, and rejoice even with joy and singing: the glory of Lebanon shall be given unto it, the excellency of Carmel and Sharon, they shall see the glory of the* LORD, *[and] the excellency of our God.*

Strengthen ye the weak hands, and confirm the feeble knees. Say to them [that are] of a fearful heart, Be strong, fear not: behold, your God will come [with] vengeance, [even] God [with] a recompence; he will come and save you. Then the eyes of the blind shall be opened, and the ears of the deaf shall be unstopped. Then shall the lame [man] leap as an hart, and the tongue of the dumb sing: for in the wilderness shall waters break out, and streams in the desert. And the parched ground shall become a pool, and the thirsty land springs of water: in the habitation of dragons, where each lay, [shall be] grass with reeds and rushes. And an highway shall be there, and a way, and it shall be called The way of holiness; the unclean shall not pass over it; but it [shall be] for those: the wayfaring men, though fools, shall not err [therein]. No lion shall be there, nor [any] ravenous beast shall go up thereon, it shall not be found there; but the redeemed shall walk [there]: and the ransomed of the LORD *shall return, and come to Zion with songs and everlasting joy upon their heads: they shall obtain joy and gladness, and sorrow and sighing shall flee away."*

This is confirmed by Romans 8:20-22: *"For the creature was made subject to vanity, not willingly, but by reason of him who hath subjected [the same] in hope because the creature itself also shall be delivered from the bondage of corruption into the glorious liberty of the children of God. For we know that the whole creation groaneth and travaileth in pain together until now."* It is strange to think of creation itself stretching out its neck like an athlete at the end of a race in order to be set free. However, in this personification of the creature or creation, Paul is emphasising the earnest desire of creation to be liberated from the curse and corruption that fell upon it when Adam sinned. It will share in the glorious liberty of the children of God who will be glorified. It reflects the time of the "Jubilee" for Israel detailed in Leviticus 25, but will affect the whole world.

Adam failed in his responsibility. Jesus will not fail. He is the Perfect One crowned with glory and honour. He will restore order to this world and, as we have seen in previous verses, hand it back to God that He might be all in all.

There is, of course, another enemy who has been disarmed by Christ, namely, the devil: *"Forasmuch then as the children are partakers of flesh and blood, he also himself likewise took part of the same; that through death he might destroy him that had the power of death, that is, the devil; and deliver them who through fear of death were all their lifetime subject to bondage."*

Because of Adam's sin, this creation has been subjected to death. But as the sinless Christ has died and risen again, He has snatched the power of death from the devil (Hebrews 2:14-18). Christ now holds the keys of death and hades (Revelation 1:18).

There is another link in the chain. The names of the children of Israel were found on the precious stones of the breastplate of judgement worn by the high priest in Old Testament times. These names were listed along in accordance to the twelve tribes. This order seems to be the one found in Numbers 10.

Exodus 28:20 states that the fourth row of the gems on this breastplate began with beryl. Remembering that Hebrew reads from right to left, this means that the name upon this jewel was that of Dan. His name means 'judge'.

"Dan shall judge his people, as one of the tribes of Israel. Dan shall be a serpent by the way, an adder in the path, that

biteth the horse heels, so that his rider shall fall backward. I have waited for thy salvation, O LORD" (Genesis 49:16-18).

Dan was responsible to judge the people of his own tribe. The judgement of Christ is universal. Dan is described as one who brings others down. This he did when falling into idolatry (Judges 18:30-31). Thankfully, Christ loves righteousness and hates iniquity. He is ever faithful! He lifts up! *"A bruised reed shall he not break, and the smoking flax shall he not quench: he shall bring forth judgement unto truth"* (Isaiah 42:3).

TABLE 2:
THE NAMES ON THE BREASTPLATE OF JUDGEMENT

Zebulun Levi	Issachar	Judah
Carbuncle	Topaz	Sardius
Dwelling	*He who is hired*	*Praise*
Gad	**Simeon**	**Reuben**
Diamond	Sapphire	Emerald
A troop/ Good fortune	*Hearing*	*Behold a son*
Benjamin	**Manasseh**	**Ephraim**
Amethyst	Agate	Ligure
Son of my right hand	*One causing forgetfulness*	*Fruitful*
Naphtali	**Asher**	**Dan**
Jasper	Onyx	Beryl
My wrestling	*Fortunate/Happy*	*Judge*

Dan is a lion's whelp who leaps from Bashan. So he pounced upon a smaller country in Joshua 19:47. The Lord Jesus subdues all His enemies, but secures those who are His own.

In Ezekiel 1:15-16 four living creatures are revealed each having the likeness of a man. Next to them were wheels that were the colour of a beryl. The chapter speaks of judgement, the living creatures being executors of God's judgement.

In Ezekiel 28:13 we find the King of Tyrus – a picture of Satan – covered with precious stones including the beryl. He is described as being full of wisdom and perfect in beauty. He was an "anointed cherub" – a protector of God's presence. He became full of himself and was cast down by God. So the stones are expressive of wisdom and beauty. Christ is the perfection of both but with humility.

In Daniel 10:6 a messenger who came with the appearance of a man had a body *"like the beryl, and his face as the appearance of lightning, and his eyes as lamps of fire, and his arms and his feet like in colour to polished brass, and the voice of his words like the voice of a multitude."* He confirmed the world events predicted in chapter 8 where one kingdom is superseded by another until, finally, the King of the North (Assyria) is broken by the Prince of princes.

In Revelation 21:20 the eighth foundation is described as being garnished with beryl. The number eight suggests super abundance, a new beginning or an eternal day – a day when: *"The pleasure of the Lord shall prosper in his hand"* (Isaiah 53:10).

9. HIS BELLY

"His belly [is as] bright ivory overlaid [with] sapphires." (Song 5:14)

In the following section, we will consider the symbolic meaning linked with:

a. his belly;

b. bright ivory; and,

c. sapphires.

A. HIS BELLY

The Hebrew word for 'belly' means 'bowels' also. The latter are associated with progeny and deep-seated emotions.

a. Progeny

Genesis 15:4 describes the bowels as instrumental in the bringing forth of children: *"And, behold, the word of the LORD [came] unto him, saying, This shall not be thine heir; but he that shall come forth out of thine own bowels shall be thine heir."*

This is confirmed by 2 Samuel 7:12: *"And when thy days be fulfilled, and thou shalt sleep with thy fathers, I will set up thy seed after thee, which shall proceed out of thy bowels, and I will establish his kingdom."*

It may be asked, "How can you apply this to Christ?" Yet when we examine Hebrews 2:11-13 we read: *"For both he that sanctifieth and they who are sanctified [are] all of one; for which cause he is not ashamed to call them brethren, saying...Behold, I and the children whom God hath given me."*

The words of Isaiah 53:10-11 also reveal the fact that Christ has a seed: *"Yet it pleased the LORD to bruise him; he hath put [him] to grief: when thou shalt make his soul an offering for sin, he shall see [his] seed, he shall prolong [his] days, and the pleasure of the LORD shall prosper in his hand. He shall see of the travail of his soul [and] shall be satisfied...".* This seed is the direct result of His soul being made an offering for sin. Those who acknowledge by faith the greatness of His person as Son of God, and appreciate in a personal way the value and effect of His sacrifice are His seed. They are the fruit of the travail of His soul. A woman suffers in her travail to bear children. Christ suffered upon the cross in order to gain His.

b. Deep-Seated Emotion

The deep grief that is associated with loss and destruction is expressed by Jeremiah in Lamentations 2:11: *"Mine eyes do fail with tears, my bowels are troubled, my liver is poured upon the earth, for the destruction of the daughter of my people; because the children and the sucklings swoon in the streets of the city."*

The deep yearning of love is expressed by Moses as Joseph meets with Benjamin again. *"And Joseph made haste; for his bowels did yearn upon his brother: and he sought [where] to weep; and he entered into [his] chamber, and wept there"* (Genesis 43:30). Most people will have experienced this kind of yearning. It is linked with a queasy feeling in the abdomen that rises up through the body to generate weeping.

In the Song of Songs 5:4 we find the yearning of love of the bride for her beloved: *"My beloved put in his hand by the hole [of the door], and my bowels were moved for him."*

How deeply the loving mother yearned for her baby son when Solomon had commanded the child to be cut in half and shared between the two women who were claiming him as their own: *"Then spake the woman whose the living child [was] unto the king, for her bowels yearned upon her son, and she said, O my lord, give her the living child, and in no wise slay it. But the other said, Let it be neither mine nor thine, [but] divide [it]"* (1 Kings 3:26). The woman expressing the emotion was, of course, the true parent. The child was saved and returned to her arms.

Paul expresses a similar yearning for the saints at Philippi: *"For God is my record, how greatly I long after you all in the bowels of Jesus Christ"* (Philippians 1:8).

Elsewhere in the New Testament, we find bowels of mercies: *"Put on therefore, as the elect of God, holy and beloved, bowels of mercies, kindness, humbleness of mind, meekness, longsuffering..."* (Colossians 3:12). These "bowels of mercies" may be rendered 'a heart of compassion' (RV). They were seen perfectly in Christ. Therefore, they speak of the pitying love that should mark Christians who would seek to empathise with, support and provide for those in need. This is confirmed by 1 John 3:17: *"But whoso hath this world's good, and seeth his brother have need, and shutteth up his bowels [of compassion] from him, how dwelleth the love of God in him?"*

Compassion is central to our God. Jeremiah knew this when he penned the words of Lamentations 3:22: *"[It is of] the LORD's mercies that we are not consumed, because his compassions fail not."* David's prayer in Psalm 86 expresses the same thought in verse 15: *"But thou, O Lord, [art] a God full of compassion, and gracious, longsuffering, and plenteous in mercy and truth."*

The same qualities mark David's greater Son, our Lord Jesus Christ, the Son of the living God. In Matthew 15:32 Jesus said, *"I have compassion on the multitude..."* The word for 'compassion' here is literally 'to have the bowels of yearning' (Young). When our Lord saw the woman who had previously lost her husband now carry her only son to his grave, He had the same compassion upon her (Luke 7:13). He touched the bier and commanded the deceased to rise. He did. But the words that follow are very precious: *"And he delivered him to his mother."* It is the same compassion that will flow from Christ as the Chief Shepherd when He reigns in a day to come.

B. BRIGHT IVORY

The Hebrew word for 'bright' has the meaning of 'prepared' or 'shining'. The main source of ivory is the elephant. In order to obtain it, there has to be a death or, at least, suffering. We are reminded of the words of the Lord Jesus Christ recorded in Luke 24:26: *"Ought not Christ to have suffered these things, and to enter into his glory?"*

We may go on to read Romans 3:24-25: *"Being justified freely by his grace through the redemption that is in Christ Jesus: whom God hath set forth [to be] a propitiation through faith in his blood, to declare his righteousness for the remission of sins that are past, through the forbearance of God..."* The thought behind 'propitiation' is the Old Testament mercy seat. There the sprinkled blood of the sin offering turned a throne of judgement into a throne of mercy, and a throne of justice into a throne of grace. It is through Christ that God is able to show mercy to the sinner who believes. The publican who cried, "God be merciful to me a sinner!" seemed to know this because the word for 'merciful' is related to the word for 'mercy seat'. The throne of

CHRIST IS MY BELOVED

grace is accessible to Christians today: *"Let us therefore come boldly unto the throne of grace, that we may obtain mercy and find grace to help in time of need"* (Hebrews 4:16).

Psalm 22 expresses the feelings of Christ during the crucifixion. The words, *"My heart is become like wax; it is melted in the midst of my bowels"* (verse 14, N.Tr.) show the depth of His pain as He hung there as our substitute.

Interestingly, it was the throne of Solomon that was made from ivory: *"Moreover the king made a great throne of ivory, and overlaid it with the best gold"* (1 Kings 10:18). Justice and judgement are the habitation of God's throne (Psalm 89:14), mercy and truth go before His face. Solomon's throne was to reflect the throne of God. So, it will be in that day to come when Christ shall rule with justice and judgement tempered with compassion.

Furthermore, ivory speaks of wealth. 2 Chronicles 9:21 reminds us that it was a precious item for trade: *"For the king's ships went to Tarshish with the servants of Huram: every three years once came the ships of Tarshish bringing gold, and silver, ivory, and apes, and peacocks."* Psalm 45:8 shows that it expresses the wealth of kings: *"All thy garments [smell] of myrrh, and aloes, [and] cassia, out of the ivory palaces, whereby they have made thee glad."*

Since the "ivory" itself speaks of the sufferings of Christ, then we can see that "ivory palaces" would represent the glory that followed those sufferings. The saying of Revelation 5:12 outlines this glory: *"Worthy is the Lamb that was slain to receive power, and riches, and wisdom, and strength, and honour, and glory, and blessing."*

C. SAPPHIRES

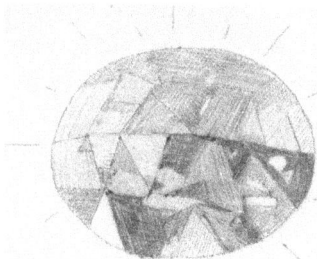

The sapphire is the second hardest stone in the world. The word comes from the Hebrew *sappir* which means 'to scratch or polish'. It is deep blue in colour. In the governmental judgement of God found in Ezekiel chapters 1 and 10 we find a sapphire-coloured (blue) platform in the likeness of a throne above the heads of the cherubim. The cherubim are "those grasped" by the throne of God. They protect His presence.

The blue reminds us of the ribband sewn into the fringes of a Jew's garment. This reminded them of all the commandments of the Lord, and to do them (Numbers 15:38). If we apply this to Christ, we immediately see that He is the One who delights to do the will of God (Psalm 40:8).

In Exodus 24:10 we find that sapphire is the heavenly colour: *"And they saw the God of Israel: and [there was] under his feet as it were a paved work of a sapphire stone, and as it were the body of heaven in [his] clearness."* This reminds us of that scripture relating to Christ in 1 Corinthians 15:47, *"The second man [is] the Lord from heaven."* He is a different kind of man altogether. As already seen, Adam, the first man, failed in His responsibility to God. As a result sin came into this world with judgement on its heels. On the other hand, the Lord Jesus, as the last Adam, fulfilled every responsiblility towards God. Righteousness had been seen in a man in this world and blessing was hard on its heels.

Philippians 2 reveals His stoop into manhood. *"Let this mind be in you which was also in Christ Jesus: who, being in the form of God, thought it not robbery to be equal with God: but made himself of no reputation, and took upon him the form of a servant, and was made in the likeness of men: and being found in fashion as a man, he humbled himself, and became obedient unto death, even the death of the cross"* (verses 5-8).

He was truly man in spirit, soul and body. From the cross He commended His spirit to God (Luke 23:46). He could say that His soul was exceeding sorrowful even unto death (Matthew 26:38). We can read of a body being prepared for Him (Hebrews 10:5). He was tempted in all these points, but found faithful (Hebrews 4:15). This is the reason that He is a sympathetic High Priest. One who has passed through the heavens. Just as a blue robe was worn by the high priest in the days of the wilderness journeys of Israel, so our great High Priest is marked out as fulfilling that office today.

In Exodus 28:18 we read that a sapphire was the second stone in the second row of the high priest's breastplate. It was engraved with the name of Simeon which means 'hearing'. There are a number of references to "ears" in scripture that refer to Christ:

a. The Digged Ear (Psalm 40:6);

b. An Opened Ear (Isaiah 50:5); and,

c. A Bored Ear (Exodus 21:6).

a. The Digged Ear (Psalm 40:6)

"Sacrifice and offering thou didst not desire; mine ears hast thou opened: burnt offering and sin offering hast thou not required."

In the verse, the literal meaning of 'opened' is 'digged'. It speaks of the body that was prepared for the Son of God. In Hebrews 10:4-10, we find, *"For [it is] not possible that the blood of bulls and of goats should take away sins. Wherefore when he cometh into the world, he saith, Sacrifice and offering thou wouldest not, but a body hast thou prepared me."* That body was prepared for the suffering of death (Hebrews 10:12). It was in that body that He bore our sins on the tree (1 Peter 2:24).

b. An Opened Ear (Isaiah 50:5)

"The Lord GOD hath opened mine ear, and I was not rebellious, neither turned away back."

In this verse we find the attitude of the disciple who seeks to do the will of His teacher. Hebrews 10:6-10 emphasise this as applying especially to Christ: *"In burnt offerings and [sacrifices] for sin thou hast had no pleasure. Then said I, Lo, I come (in the volume of the book it is written of me,) to do thy will, O God. Above when he said, Sacrifice and offering and burnt offerings and [offering] for sin thou wouldest not, neither hadst pleasure [therein]; which are offered by the law; then said he, Lo, I come to do thy will, O God. He taketh away the first, that he may establish the second. By the which will we are sanctified through the offering of the body of Jesus Christ once [for all]."*

c. A Bored Ear (Exodus 21:5-6)

"And if the servant shall plainly say, I love my master, my wife, and my children; I will not go out free: then his master shall bring him unto the judges; he shall also bring him to the door, or unto the door post; and his master shall bore his ear through with an aul; and he shall serve him for ever."

1. Loving the Master

Applying this to the Lord Jesus, we can see that He loved His Master (His Father). John 14:31 records His words, *"But that the world may know that I love the Father; and as the Father gave me commandment, even so I do. Arise, let us go hence."* The measure of Christ's love for His Father was His obedience. Here, the cross was before Him. Of course, the love of the Son for the Father was reciprocated. In John 17:24 we find that the Lord Jesus knew this: *"Father, [as to] those whom thou hast given me, I desire that where I am they also may be with me, that they may behold my glory which thou hast given me, for thou lovedst me before [the] foundation of [the] world"* (N.Tr.).

2. Loving the Wife

Ephesians 5:25-27 commands: *"Husbands, love your wives, even as Christ also loved the church, and gave himself for it; that he might sanctify and cleanse it with the washing of water by the word, that he might present it to himself a glorious church, not having spot, or wrinkle, or any such thing; but that it should be holy and without blemish."* Christ loved the church so much that He delivered up Himself to death for it. Husbands, do we really love our wives as much as this? How easy it would be for Christian wives to submit to their husbands if husbands loved as Christ did.

3. Loving the Children

Hebrews 2:10-13 reveal that our Lord has children: *"For it became him, for whom [are] all things, and by whom are all things, in bringing many sons unto glory, to make the captain of their salvation perfect through sufferings. For both he that sanctifieth and they who are sanctified [are] all of one: for which cause he is not ashamed to call them brethren, saying, I will declare thy name unto my brethren, in the midst of the church will I sing praise unto thee. And again, I will put my trust in him. And again, Behold I and the children which God hath given me."*

His Nazariteship is also linked to the sapphire in Lamentations 4:7, while beauty is again linked to the sapphire in Ezekiel 28:13. In Revelation 21:19, the second foundation stone was of sapphire. The number two indicates a *difference* or *another* with reference to bad or good. For example, it may speak of division and, on the other hand, speak of witness. When Christ came into this world, His light dispelled the darkness. He witnessed to His Father by manifesting and declaring His name (John 17:6 & 26). Yet the people who heard His teaching were often divided in their belief.

10. HIS LEGS

"His legs [are as] pillars of marble, set upon sockets of fine gold." (Song 5:15)

In this section, we will examine the scriptural meanings of:

  a. legs;
  b. pillars of marble; and,
  c. sockets of fine gold.

A. LEGS

Most of the references to "legs" in the Bible surround animals that were to be offered to God as burnt offerings. The legs of these creatures were "washed with water" usually along with the inwards: *"But his inwards and his legs shall he wash in water: and the priest shall burn all on the altar, [to be] a burnt sacrifice, an offering made by fire, of a sweet savour unto the LORD"* (Leviticus 1:9). The action of washing is typical of the effect of the application the word of God to the soul. It is that whereby a man shall be born

159

again (John 3:5). It is that which cleanses morally (Psalm 119:9). The Lord Jesus said that His disciples were clean through the word He spoke to them (John 15:3). This idea of cleanness is symbolised by legs in Leviticus 11:21: *"Yet these may ye eat of every flying creeping thing that goeth upon [all] four, which have legs above their feet, to leap withal upon the earth…"* That which was clean had legs above their feet.

Of course, the burnt offerings refer to the perfection of Christ in His sacrifice. The work He did at the cross rose as a sweet fragrance to God. The inwards speak of every motive of Christ being in accordance with the will of God. The legs indicate that His walk and warfare were also according to the word of God. Warfare is suggested because of the exhortation for Christians to "stand" in Ephesians 6: *"Finally, my brethren, be strong in the Lord, and in the power of his might. Put on the whole armour of God, that ye may be able to stand against the wiles of the devil. For we wrestle not against flesh and blood, but against principalities, against powers, against the rulers of the darkness of this world, against spiritual wickedness in high [places]. Wherefore take unto you the whole armour of God, that ye may be able to withstand in the evil day, and having done all, to stand. Stand therefore, having your loins girt about with truth, and having on the breastplate of righteousness; and your feet shod with the preparation of the gospel of peace; above all, taking the shield of faith, wherewith ye shall be able to quench all the fiery darts of the wicked. And take the helmet of salvation, and the sword of the Spirit, which is the word of God: Praying always with all prayer and supplication in the Spirit, and watching thereunto with all perseverance and supplication for all saints"* (verses 10-18).

In this spiritual battle, the Lord Jesus was always strong in His God and in the power of His might. He has spoiled the devil (bound the strong man – Matthew 12:29). He is Lord of all!

B. As Pillars of Marble

If we trace the use of pillars through the Bible, we find that they are used for:

a. the presence of the Lord;

b. God's house;

c. witness; and

d. strong supports.

a. The Presence of the Lord

In Numbers 14:14 we clearly see that the pillar of cloud and pillar of fire reveal the presence of God: *"And they will tell [it] to the inhabitants of this land: [for] they have heard that thou LORD [art] among this people, that thou LORD art seen face to face, and [that] thy cloud standeth over them, and [that] thou goest before them, by day time in a pillar of a cloud, and in a pillar of fire by night."* Standing over the people, it showed that God was their Protector – He was for them. Going before them reminds us that God was their Shepherd. The One who sustains, cares and guides.

In applying this to the Lord Jesus, we see Him as the Chief Shepherd – the One who arises as the Sun of righteousness with healing in His wings. In Exodus 13:21 we read, *"And the LORD went before them by day in a pillar of a cloud, to lead them the way; and by night in a pillar of fire, to give them light; to go by day and night…"* Here again we see the Lord leading as the Shepherd, but He is also the light-giver. We know from John 1:9-13 that the Lord Jesus is the True Light: *"[That] was the true Light, which lighteth every man that cometh into the world. He was in the world, and the world was made by him, and the world knew him not. He came unto his own, and his own received him not. But as many as received him, to them gave he power to become the sons of God, [even] to them that believe on his name: which were born, not of blood, nor of the will of the flesh, nor of the will of man, but of God."* The Lord, who dispelled darkness, is the authority whereby people who receive Him become children of God. Those who follow Christ have the light of life because He is the Light of the world.

Furthermore, in Numbers 12:5 we find: *"And the LORD came down in the pillar of the cloud, and stood [in] the door of the tabernacle, and called Aaron and Miriam: and they both came forth."* Here the Lord intervenes when Aaron and Miriam state that He has not only spoken through Moses, but also through them. They are called by God to the tabernacle and rebuked. The Lord told them that He spoke in visions or dreams to the prophets, but emphasises that He spoke with Moses face to face and that Moses could see His form. What will it be to stand face to face with Christ and see His form?

In a way, the disciples, Peter, James and John, had this privilege on the Mount of Transfiguration. *"While he yet spake, behold, a bright cloud overshadowed them: and behold a voice out of the cloud, which said, This is my beloved Son, in whom I am well pleased; hear ye him"* (Matthew 17:5). The Shekinah Glory – the Excellent Glory – overshadowed them. We know that this was the presence of God the Father because 2 Peter 1:17 tells us *"For he received from God the Father honour and glory, when there came such a voice to him from the excellent glory, This is my beloved Son, in whom I am well pleased."* The preview of the coming kingdom showed Christ glorified. As ever, He was the Son of the Father's love. He will rule as such.

Interestingly, a cloud received the Lord Jesus when He ascended into heaven. This shows that He was entirely approved of by God (Acts 1:9). At the end of Luke's Gospel, we see Him carried up to heaven. The Father was bearing up His dependent Son. In the day of the kingdom to come, the Lord Jesus will be there. God will be present because His name shall be called The Mighty God!

b. God's House

A pillar can also represent God's house. In Genesis 28:18, 22 we read, *"And Jacob rose up early in the morning, and took the stone that he had put [for] his pillows, and set it up [for] a pillar, and poured oil upon the top of it. … And this stone, which I have set [for] a pillar, shall be God's house: and of all that thou shalt give me I will surely give the tenth unto thee."* The Lord had spoken to Jacob during the night. He had promised to go with him, to keep him and to bring him back to that place. Jacob was disturbed by the fact that the Lord was there. He set up a pillar of stone and anointed it with oil calling the place Bethel because it was the house of God and the gate of heaven. Jacob then promised that the Lord would be his God if He kept His word and brought him back to his father's house.

Today, we know that the House of God is composed of believers in the Lord Jesus Christ. This is confirmed by 1 Timothy 3:15: *"But if I tarry long, that thou mayest know how thou oughtest to behave thyself in the house of God, which is the church of the living God, the pillar and ground of the truth."* In this verse, we have reference to the house of God as the pillar of truth. It is that which bears a full and immovable witness to the full revelation that God has given.

In a similar manner, Revelation 3:12 reveals that an individual overcomer in the faith has a place as a pillar in the house of God: *"Him that overcometh will I make a pillar in the temple of my God, and he shall go no more out: and I will write upon him the name of my God, and the name of the city of my God, [which is] new Jerusalem, which cometh down out of heaven from my God: and [I will write upon him] my new name."* As such, the believer is a stable witness to the name of God and to that of His city. The word "temple" in the verse speaks of the "inner sanctuary" – the place of God's presence. What a privilege! Let us also remember, as previously mentioned, that Christ is the Son over His own house.

c. Witness

We have already touched on the fact that pillars speak of witness in the passages above, but we can see it clearly stated in Genesis 31:52 where Laban and Jacob come to terms of peace: *"This heap [be] witness, and [this] pillar [be] witness, that I will not pass over this heap to thee, and that thou shalt not pass over this heap and this pillar unto me, for harm."*

In 1 Kings 7:15, we find that Hiram from Tyre cast two bronze pillars for Solomon's temple. There seemed to be no use for these in the temple's structure because they stood in front of it. However, verse 21 tells us that the one on the right was called Jachin and the one on the left Boaz. Jachin means 'He shall establish' and Boaz means 'In him is strength'. This shows that the Lord is the one who sets up the Kingdom of God and has the strength to maintain it. I have a personal feeling that these two pillars also had the function of being lamps. Hence, the bowls in the chapiters. In that day to come, the Lord Jesus will be, as ever, the faithful witness. He will establish and keep His people.

d. Strong Supports

Judges 16:26 reveals the obvious – pillars were supports in the construction of buildings. *"And Samson said unto the lad that held him by the hand, Suffer me that I may feel the pillars whereupon the house standeth, that I may lean upon them."* The lad answered the request of Samson who proceeded to dislodge, with renewed strength, the pillars and to slay the mocking Philistines.

In the New Testament, the word "pillar" is used to describe spiritual men who steadfastly support the church of God. Galatians 2:9 reveals, *"And when James, Cephas, and John, who seemed to be pillars, perceived the grace that was given unto me, they gave to me and Barnabas the right hands of fellowship; that we [should go] unto the heathen, and they unto the circumcision."* Oh, that we might be faithful witnesses to God and His work and sturdy pillars in His house here on earth knowing that the Lord Jesus is its builder and foundation!

C. SOCKETS OF FINE GOLD

It must be noted that the word for "fine gold" here is not the same as that for the head which is described as "most fine gold". Psalm 19:10 tells us that fine gold was desirable, but the judgements of the Lord were more so: *"More to be desired [are they] than gold, yea, than much fine gold."* Psalm 119:127 shows that fine gold was loved, but no so much as the commandments of the Lord: *"Therefore I love thy commandments above gold; yea, above fine gold."*

In Proverbs 8:19 we find that wisdom has a fruit that is better than gold, yea, than fine gold. The merchandise of wisdom brings a gain that is better than fine gold (Proverbs 3:14). However, it is in Proverbs 25:12 where we have a direct comparison: *"[As] an earring of gold, and an ornament of fine gold, [so is] a wise reprover upon an obedient ear."* Now here is someone to be desired and loved – a wise reprover. There is only One who does this perfectly, namely, the Lord Jesus Christ. Is He not the Person to whom Isaiah 13:12 points: *"I will make a man more precious than fine gold; even a man than the golden wedge of Ophir."* And, of course, He is the most precious son of Zion. *"The precious sons of Zion, comparable to fine gold..."* (Lamentations 4:2).

Here we have the Lion of the tribe of Judah – the King of kings. He will reign in wisdom (Proverbs 8:15) because He is Wisdom. In Christ is seen perfectly that wisdom which is from above – that which *is pure, then peaceable, gentle, [and] easy to be intreated, full of mercy and good fruits, without partiality, and without hypocrisy* (James 3:17).

In Proverbs 8 we see the wisdom of God in Christ by the Spirit. There He reproves, speaks in righteousness, and instructs. He is prudent, counsels and provides understanding. He loves. With Him is wealth. Wisdom is eternal, yet His delights were with the sons of men. Those who find Him find life and obtain favour of the Lord.

In the above chapter Wisdom is presented in the feminine because that is how it is classed in the Hebrew language, just as we refer to a ship as "she" in our language. When the female is used in relation to Christ then the effect is manward. The female offerings are for man's blessing. The male is usually used for God's pleasure or purpose. So the whole character of our Lord Jesus Christ is based upon wisdom.

11. His Countenance

"His countenance [is] as Lebanon, excellent as the cedars." (Song 5:15)

In this section, we will consider:

a. what is meant by his countenance;

b. the relevance of Lebanon; and,

c. the excellence of cedars.

A. What is meant by his countenance?

The Hebrew word for 'countenance' in this verse is *mareh*. It is translated in a variety of ways depending on the context of the passage. For example, it is used many times for *appearance*, *sight* and *vision*, while in other places it is used more rarely for *visage*, *beauty*, *form* and *pattern*.

In Judges 13:6 we find that it relates to general appearance: *"Then the woman came and told her husband, saying, A man of God came unto me, and his countenance [was] like the countenance of an angel of God, very terrible: but I asked him not whence he [was], neither told he me his name..."*

1 Samuel 16:7 shows that the Lord places little importance on the outward appearance: *"But the LORD said unto Samuel, Look not on his countenance, or on the height of his stature; because I have refused him: for [the LORD seeth] not as man seeth; for man looketh on the outward appearance, but the LORD looketh on the heart."*

Interestingly, David must have had both outward and inward beauty because we read in 1 Samuel 16:12: *"And he sent, and brought him in. Now he [was] ruddy, [and] withal of a beautiful countenance, and goodly to look to. And the* LORD *said, Arise, anoint him: for this [is] he."*

It is this aspect of the king's beauty which is the focus in our verse concerning the bridegroom in the Song of Songs. When we apply this to the King of kings, we can see the beauty of the Lord as recorded at the time of His transfiguration: *"And as he prayed, the fashion of his countenance was altered, and his raiment [was] white [and] glistering"* (Luke 9:29). At the same time, we find Matthew describing His second coming as lightning: *"For as the lightning cometh out of the east, and shineth even unto the west; so shall also the coming of the Son of man be"* (Matthew 24:27).

While our Lord Jesus Christ was on earth, the words of Isaiah 53:2 applied to Him: *"And when we shall see him, [there is] no beauty that we should desire him."* For some reason, there seemed to be no beauty in the outward appearance in the Lord Jesus that would have made Him popular and desirable. In John 8 Jesus spoke the words, *"Before Abraham was, I am"* (verse 58) in response to the Jews saying, *"Thou art not yet fifty years old, and hast thou seen Abraham?"* Of course, Jesus was claiming to be Yahweh – the I AM. Not only did He exist before Abraham, He existed as God. But the words: *"Thou art not yet fifty years old"* suggest that the Lord Jesus looked older than a man in his early thirties. Life on earth, in the steadfast service of God, seems to have taken its toll on the appearance of the man Christ Jesus. However, in that day to come, His countenance will be lovely, even surpassing the appearance of Daniel and his friends in the court of Nebuchadnezzar (Daniel 1:13).

In the Old Testament, we find that the face of Moses shone when he had been in the presence of the Lord to

receive the Law. *"But if the ministration of death, written [and] engraven in stones, was glorious, so that the children of Israel could not stedfastly behold the face of Moses for the glory of his countenance..."* (2 Corinthians 3:7). This was a passing glory. The face of the risen Lord Jesus Christ is described in 2 Corinthians 4:6, *"For God, who commanded the light to shine out of darkness, hath shined in our hearts, to [give] the light of the knowledge of the glory of God in the face of Jesus Christ."* Christ is the image of God (verse 4). He will be seen in all His beauty. The glory of God will permanently radiate from Him. Yet, of the same One, it is written, *"His visage was so marred more than any man, and his form more than the sons of men"* (Isaiah 52:14). When He hung upon Calvary's cross, it was difficult to discern that Christ was even a man so badly was He disfigured by wicked hands. God will soon give His answer to that.

When depicted as the Judge in the early chapters of Revelation, it is written of our Lord, *"And he had in his right hand seven stars: and out of his mouth went a sharp twoedged sword: and his countenance [was] as the sun shineth in his strength"* (Revelation 1:16). Such will be His physical radiance in that day to come. The Man of Sorrows will be a Man of Joy. The One who saw no corruption will have fulness of joy in the presence of God (Psalm 16:11; compare Acts 2:28).

Throughout Scripture, the countenance also reveals the mood of the person. It may be sad, fierce, angry or favourable. One example is found in Matthew 6:16: *"Moreover when ye fast, be not, as the hypocrites, of a sad countenance: for they disfigure their faces, that they may appear unto men to fast. Verily I say unto you, They have their reward."* In the day of His kingdom, His appearance will be one of favour towards His own and one of fierceness towards His enemies.

The countenance of Yahweh is seen in Numbers 6:26. When He lifts up His countenance, it is to give peace. Christ is the Prince of Peace.

B. AS LEBANON

Lebanon is a mountain range in Syria. The Hebrew word for Lebanon means 'white', 'snowy' or 'incense'. This whiteness again reminds us of the countenance of Christ at His transfiguration where His face shone as the sun and His raiment was as white as the light (Matthew 17:2). This was a picture of His future glory as the King of kings and Lord of lords. Moses and Elijah were present on that mountain with the Lord. But it was not in regard to them that the Father spoke from the cloud. It was to direct the disciples' gaze to His beloved Son: *"This is my beloved Son, in whom I am well pleased; hear ye him"* (verse 5). The disciples were directed to hear Christ above the Law of Moses and the Old Testament prophets. The Son had the seal of God's authority. This is supported by Hebrews 1:1-2: *"God...hath in these last days spoken unto us by [his] Son..."* In that future millennial day, He will be the King with sovereign authority.

Psalm 92:12 reminds us that the righteous grow like a cedar in Lebanon. Our Lord is Jesus Christ the righteous. He is the Lord our righteousness (*Yahweh Tsidkenu*).

In Song of Solomon 4:15 we read, *"A fountain of gardens, a well of living waters, and streams from Lebanon."* Living water symbolises the Holy Spirit actively giving life. The fact that Lebanon contains many of these reveals that Christ is the Life-giver. He is the Person in whom the

Holy Spirit of God dwells. The characteristics of that Spirit mark Him out (Isaiah 11:2) as does the fruit of the Spirit (Galatians 5:22).

Isaiah 60:13 states: *"The glory of Lebanon shall come unto thee, the fir tree, the pine tree, and the box together, to beautify the place of my sanctuary; and I will make the place of my feet glorious."* The excellence of Lebanon is its timber. It was used in the building of the temple – God's dwelling place among men. So the beauty of the Lord Jesus is not only suitable for the presence of God, it enhances its beauty. We have already mentioned the cedar, but here we find the pine, fir and box trees. The glory of the Lord is linked with these, for Isaiah 35:2 informs us: *"It shall blossom abundantly, and rejoice even with joy and singing: the glory of Lebanon shall be given unto it, the excellency of Carmel and Sharon, they shall see the glory of the LORD, [and] the excellency of our God."*

The wood of the pine was used to make booths during the celebration of the Feast of Tabernacles. This feast is a picture of the millennial period of blessing (Nehemiah 8:15). Furthermore, Isaiah 41:19 (which also refers to the box tree) relates to the blessing of the Lord seen in the turning of Israel's barren land into fruitfulness.

The fir tree was used in the making of musical instruments which were, in turn, used in praise of the Lord (2 Samuel 6:5). This reminds us that the Lord Jesus is the leader of praise in the assembly (Hebrews 2:12). It was also used in the making of the temple doors reminding us that He is the door who gives salvation, liberty and life (John 10:9). In Isaiah 55:13, we find that it is also a sign of the Lord's blessing reminding us that every gift from God comes with our Lord Jesus Christ (Romans 8:32).

Hosea 14:5 shows that under the favourable hand of the
Lord, Israel was to grow as the lily and cast forth his roots
as Lebanon. These roots show that Israel will have stabil-
ity and fruitfulness under the hand of God.

Of course, the most obvious meaning of His countenance
being as Lebanon would relate to the overall appearance
of majesty seen in the mountains of Lebanon. The glory
of the Lord Jesus Christ as the King will surpass that of
Solomon.

C. AS EXCELLENT AS THE CEDARS

The word "excellent" has the force of "chosen" which
reminds us that the Lord Jesus Christ is elect and precious. He is the chosen Messiah.

As already quoted in chapter two:

> *Father, how precious unto Thee*
> *Is Thy beloved Son,*
> *In whom Thou dost perfection see,*
> *Thy holy, blessed One!*
> *etc.*

Ezekiel 31:3 seems to be a parallel to this description:
*"Behold, the Assyrian [was] a cedar in Lebanon with fair
branches, and with a shadowing shroud, and of an high
stature; and his top was among the thick boughs."* Here the
Assyrian is outlined as one of the mighty ones (cedar)
being handsome (fair branches), protective (shadowing
shroud) and majestic (high stature). All these apply to the
Lord Jesus in a far greater way.

In fact, this description of the countenance of the
Shepherd King is summed up in Isaiah 32:1-2: *"Behold, a
king shall reign in righteousness, and princes shall rule in
judgement. And a man shall be as a hiding place from the
wind, and a covert from the tempest; as rivers of water in a*

dry place, as the shadow of a great rock in a weary land." (See pages 20-22.)

12. HIS MOUTH

"His mouth [is] most sweet." (Song 5:16)

The Hebrew word for 'mouth' here means 'palate' or 'taste' while the word 'sweet' literally means 'sweet things'. Psalm 119:103 contains the thoughts of taste and sweetness. *"How sweet are thy words unto my taste! [yea, sweeter] than honey to my mouth!"* Moreover, *"If I do not remember thee, let my tongue cleave to the roof of my mouth; if I prefer not Jerusalem above my chief joy"* (Psalm 137:6, probably written by Daniel). Thus the words of God are received. They are sweet to the writer. If we apply this to the Lord Jesus, we find these words: *"Believest thou not that I am in the Father, and the Father in me? the words that I speak unto you I speak not of myself: but the Father that dwelleth in me, he doeth the works"* (John 14:10). Christ attributes His words as being those of His Father. This is made clear by verse 24 of the same chapter: *"He that loveth me not keepeth not my sayings: and the word which ye hear is not mine, but the Father's which sent me."* The Lord was able to taste for Himself the words of the Father before breathing them out to men. So we see Him as the Mediator between God and men, the man Christ Jesus (1 Timothy 2:5).

Job 9:33 speaks of the daysman (one to reason): *"Neither is there any daysman betwixt us, [that] might lay his hand upon us both."* As He is God and Man, the Lord Jesus Christ was able to reach up to God and out to men. He was therefore, perfectly qualified to act as a go-between or mediator. He still pleads our cause in heaven as our Great High Priest and our Advocate.

He is also the Mediator of the New Covenant: *"But now hath he obtained a more excellent ministry, by how much also he is the mediator of a better covenant, which was established upon better promises"* (Hebrews 8:6). The Jewish believers addressed in Hebrews needed to have the assurance that Christ brought them a better covenant than that of the Law of Moses (Galatians 3:19) and a covenant with greater promises than those of Leviticus 26. So Christ is a more excellent mediator than Moses. He brings with Him a better covenant that is grounded in His sacrifice (Hebrews 10:29 and 13:20) and leads to glory.

The epistle to the Hebrews outlines at least ten things that are now "better". They include:

- 1:4 – better than angels;
- 6:9 – better things;
- 7:1-9 – better than Abraham;
- 7:19 – better hope;
- 7:22 – better covenant;
- 8:6 – better promises;
- 9:23 – better sacrifices;
- 10:34 – better possession;
- 1:16 – better country; and,
- 11:35 – better resurrection.

The Mosaic Covenant was dependent upon the people's obedience. This New Covenant was based upon the grace of God. There was a New Covenant promised to Israel (Jeremiah 31:31) and Ezekiel speaks of the spiritual rebirth of the nation of Israel in chapter 36 and, in that day, the beauty of Jerusalem will be restored. She will once again reflect the comeliness of the Lord (Ezekiel 16). We have all the blessings of the New Covenant today, and more! The promises that establish it include:

- *the Lord writing His law in their minds and hearts* (the people would have not only the knowledge of what God wanted them to do, but the desire to obey Him)

- *the Lord promising to be their God* (not just as the God of Abraham, Isaac and Jacob, but as the God of glory, love, patience, comfort, grace, hope and peace as revealed in the New Testament scriptures)

- *they would be His people again* (blessed, but responsible to live holy lives)

- *He would be known by them* (this reflects an intimacy in knowing and loving God)

- *He would be merciful to them* (meet their needs with pity and every resource available)

- *their sins and iniquities would not be remembered by Him* (no longer an annual remembrance of sin that required the sacrifice on that great Day of Atonement – the sacrifice has passed, once for all, and God can freely forgive on the basis of the blood of the New Covenant – Luke 22:20).

So Christ is also called the Mediator of the New Testament in Hebrews 9:15: *"And for this cause he is the mediator of the new testament, that by means of death, for the redemption of the transgressions [that] were under the first testament, they which are called might receive the promise of eternal inheritance."* Here we note two things in particular. First, believers in Old Testament times were redeemed by the then future death of Christ. The sacrifices of old could never take away sins; but knowing that the future death of Christ would suffice, God was able to pass those sins by, yet remain just (Rom 3:25, 26). Second, they were to receive an eternal inheritance.

175

Not all the blood of beasts
   On Jewish altars slain
Could give the guilty conscience peace,
   Or wash away its stain.

But Christ, the heavenly Lamb,
   Took all our guilt away,
A sacrifice of nobler name
   And richer blood than they.

(I. Watts)

In John 15:15 Jesus calls His disciples "friends" because they have been informed as to why He acted. We read, *"Henceforth I call you not servants; for the servant knoweth not what his lord doeth: but I have called you friends; for all things that I have heard of my Father I have made known unto you."* The revelations made by the Lord Jesus originated with the Father. In fact, the very words that were given to Christ by the Father were fully passed on to the disciples (John 17:8 and John 8:27-29). Hence, they were not just servants to obey commands, but were friends who understood the motives behind the commands. (We will examine this in a little more detail later).

So the mouth is known for receiving or tasting the word of God and then for teaching or preaching the same. This was true of the prophets of old: *"But those things, which God before had shewed by the mouth of all his prophets, that Christ should suffer, he hath so fulfilled. ... Whom the heaven must receive until the times of restitution of all things, which God hath spoken by the mouth of all his holy prophets since the world began"* (Acts 3:18, 21).

Matthew 5:2 shows that this was true of Christ: *"And he opened his mouth, and taught them..."* He is the Prophet of whom the Lord spoke in Deuteronomy 18:18: *"I will raise them up a Prophet from among their brethren, like unto thee, and will put my words in his mouth; and he shall speak unto them all that I shall command him."*

He Himself said, *"For I have not spoken from myself, but the Father who sent me has himself given me commandment what I should say and what I should speak; and I know that his commandment is life eternal. What therefore I speak, as the Father hath said to me, so I speak"* (John 12:49-50, N.Tr.).

Luke 4:22 describes the words of His mouth as being "gracious". This shows the condition of our Lord's heart because *"out of the abundance of the heart the mouth speaketh"* (Matthew 12:34). His purity is again marked by the mouth for 1 Peter 2:22 states that He *"did no sin, neither was guile found in his mouth…"*

Furthermore, Matthew 13:35 reminds us that the Lord also taught the people using parables: *"That it might be fulfilled which was spoken by the prophet, saying, I will open my mouth in parables; I will utter things which have been kept secret from the foundation of the world."* The intention of a parable was not to make teaching clear, but rather to disguise the meaning so only those with spiritual insight could understand it (Matthew 13:13-15).

Of course, when the Lord was led as a sheep to the slaughter, His submission to the will of God was marked by His silence: *"The place of the scripture which he read was this, He was led as a sheep to the slaughter; and like a lamb dumb before his shearer, so opened he not his mouth"* (Acts 8:32). Just prior to this scripture, we find the evangelist, Philip, opening his mouth to teach the Ethiopian eunuch. He went on to speak about Jesus.

Additionally, praise comes from the mouth: *"And said unto him, Hearest thou what these say? And Jesus saith unto them, Yea; have ye never read, Out of the mouth of babes and sucklings thou hast perfected praise?"* (Matthew 21:16). *"And his mouth was opened immediately, and his tongue [loosed], and he spake, and praised God"* (Luke 1:64). Hebrews 2:12 reminds us that the Lord Jesus leads the singing in the assembly. Just as Chenaniah organised the songs and music in the days of the temple – so Christ leads out worship to the Father today.

There is also a reference to the Lord "tasting" in the New Testament. It is found in Hebrews 2:9 where He tasted death for every thing. Who can fathom the sufferings of Christ except God Himself?

In 2 Corinthians 13:1 we are reminded that the mouth is a source of witness; *"This is the third [time] I am coming to you. In the mouth of two or three witnesses shall every word be established."* Two give us adequate witness. Three give us abundant witness.

However, there is a more fearful aspect to the mouth of our Lord, namely, judgement. 2 Thessalonians 2:8 reads: *"And then shall that Wicked be revealed, whom the Lord shall consume with the spirit of his mouth, and shall destroy with the brightness of his coming…"*

Revelation 1:16 and 2:16 link His mouth with a sharp two-edged sword. His word is used to judge and conquer. In Revelation 3:16 He cannot tolerate the taste of the unfaithfulness of the Laodicean church: *"So then because thou art lukewarm, and neither cold nor hot, I will spue thee out of my mouth."*

178

In Revelation 19:15 His mouth is again used as a weapon: *"And out of his mouth goeth a sharp sword, that with it he should smite the nations: and he shall rule them with a rod of iron: and he treadeth the winepress of the fierceness and wrath of Almighty God."*

13. ALTOGETHER LOVELY

"Yea, he [is] altogether lovely." (Song 5:16)

The Hebrew word used here for 'lovely' may be translated as 'desirable', 'beloved' or 'pleasant'.

What a contrast to Isaiah 53:2 which describes the Man of Sorrows having no form nor comeliness and no beauty that He should be desired! Here we find a Man of Joy whose beauty cannot be surpassed. In every aspect of the foregoing description, He has been found perfect.

As Wisdom, Christ could say: *"When he gave to the sea his decree, that the waters should not pass his commandment: when he appointed the foundations of the earth: then I was by him, [as] one brought up [with him]: and I was daily [his] delight, rejoicing always before him..."* (Proverbs 8:29-30). Therefore, as the Wisdom of God and the Power of God, His reign will be, like Himself, perfect.

Throughout the scriptures, we find that desirable things are removed from the people under a form of judgement (1 Kings 20:6; Lamentations 1:10; Isaiah 64:11). In our passage above, we find that the Lord Jesus Christ is most desirable. He will be present with Zion in that future day (The Lord is there) and bring with Him the wonderful blessing of God. Today, we are grateful for His promise to be with two or three who are gathered together in His Name.

14. My Friend

"This [is] my beloved and this [is] my friend..." (Song 5:16)

Earlier in this book we considered "The Beloved" in some detail. It is notable that the bride claims him as her own possession, 'my' beloved. It reminds us of the force of the words of Thomas to the resurrected Christ – *"...My Lord, and my God"* (John 20:28). Such will be the exclamation of the earthly bride of Christ, Zion, when He appears as the glorious King. However, the term 'Beloved' shows that her relationship to the Messiah is far more intimate. She adores Him!

The Hebrew word for 'friend' is most often translated as 'neighbour'. In Luke 10, it is recorded:

"And, behold, a certain lawyer stood up, and tempted him, saying, Master, what shall I do to inherit eternal life? He said unto him, What is written in the law? how readest thou? And he answering said, Thou shalt love the Lord thy God with all thy heart, and with all thy soul, and with all thy strength, and with all thy mind; and thy neighbour as thyself. And he said unto him, Thou hast answered right: this do, and thou shalt live. But he, willing to justify himself, said unto Jesus, And who is my neighbour?

And Jesus answering said, A certain [man] went down from Jerusalem to Jericho, and fell among thieves, which stripped him of his raiment, and wounded [him], and departed, leaving [him] half dead. And by chance there came down a certain priest that way: and when he saw him, he passed by on the other side. And likewise a Levite, when he was at the place, came and looked [on him], and passed by on the other side. But a certain Samaritan, as he journeyed, came where he was: and when he saw him, he had compassion [on him], and went to [him], and bound up his wounds, pouring in oil and wine, and set him on his own beast, and brought him to an inn, and took care of him. And on the morrow when he departed, he took out two pence, and gave [them] to the host, and said unto him, Take care of him; and whatsoever thou spendest more, when I come again, I will repay thee.

Which now of these three, thinkest thou, was neighbour unto him that fell among the thieves? And he said, He that shewed mercy on him. Then said Jesus unto him, Go, and do thou likewise" (verses 25-37).

The Lord Jesus Christ knew that the lawyer was out to trap Him, but He used the challenge to teach the lawyer a lesson by using this event of what may be termed "a mugging" to illustrate what is meant by a neighbour. The answer of the lawyer was accepted by Christ: *"He that shewed mercy on him. Then said Jesus unto him, Go, and do thou likewise."* So a neighbour is one who meets the need of another even if deemed to be an enemy (because the Jews and the Samaritans despised one another). Job 6:14 says: *"To him that is afflicted pity [should be shewed] from his friend..."*.

So a neighbour (or friend) is someone who is able to exercise compassion. In this, the Lord Jesus was Himself the perfect example.

As noted in some detail previously, Christ was moved with compassion when:

- He saw the crowds harassed and like sheep without a shepherd (Matthew 9:36);

- He touched the eyes of the blind man and gave him sight (Matthew 20:34); and,

- He found the widow of Nain bereft of her only son and brought him back to life (Luke 7:13).

The event concerning the Good Samaritan also reveals a pattern of action that the Lord Himself took. The outline below is taken from N. Crawford's *What the Bible Teaches: Luke*.

1. The Hated Name – "Samaritan" (10:33)

2. The Heavenly Blessing – "Came where he was" (10:33)

3. The Holy Companion – "took care of him" (10:34)

4. The House of Care – "Brought him to an inn" (10:34)

5. The Hope of His Return – "When I come again" (10:35).

Christ loved us and came to where we were. This entailed His becoming a man. He was despised and rejected, particularly by religious and rulers. Yet seeing our deep need of salvation, He went to the cross in order to heal us from sin. He places us in the charge of the Holy Spirit while He is absent in glory. But He will come again to take us to be with Himself!

The meaning of the Greek word for 'neighbour' is 'one who is near'. It reminds us of the word 'paraclete' ('comforter') which is used of the Spirit of God. It means 'one who comes alongside to help'. What a picture of two neighbours – Christ (the Samaritan) and the Holy Spirit (the innkeeper).

In John 15 the Lord Jesus calls His disciples 'friends': *"Greater love hath no man than this, that a man lay down his life for his friends. Ye are my friends, if ye do whatsoever I command you. Henceforth I call you not servants; for the servant knoweth not what his lord doeth: but I have called you friends; for all things that I have heard of my Father I have made known unto you"* (verses 13-15).

He contrasts friendship and service. The servant has a duty to obey the commands of his lord without question. A friend has the privilege of knowing the reason behind any command coming from his companion. Christ had revealed to the disciples the Father's love and purposes. A friend is an informed person. Hence, any disciple who is loving and obedient is a friend of the Lord Jesus. Proverbs 17:17 states *"A friend loveth at all times…"* It is worth noting that although the Lord Jesus calls His disciples His friends, He remains their Lord. He is to be obeyed.

When Judas Iscariot came to the Garden of Gethsemane to betray Jesus with a kiss, the Lord called him "friend": *"And Jesus said unto him, Friend, wherefore art thou come? Then came they, and laid hands on Jesus, and took him"* (Matthew 26:50). In the shadow of the cross and in anguish of spirit already, how this manner of betrayal must have hurt the Lord Jesus! However, in a day to come He shall have a measure of joy when identified as the pierced One: *"And [one] shall say unto him, What [are] these wounds in thine hands? Then he shall answer, [Those] with which I was wounded [in] the house of my friends"* (Zechariah 13:6).

Interestingly, the passage in John 15:13 begins with the pinnacle of human love, namely, that a man lay down his life for his friends. In a sense, we can see that the Lord was saying that if the disciples obeyed His commands then He would call them friends and not only reveal the motives behind His commands, but also lay down his life for them. We know, of course, that the love of Christ is a divine love. It is a love which prompted Him to lay down His life for His enemies (Romans 5:10). He Himself practised what He preached: *"Love ... your enemies, and do good..."* (Luke 6:35).

Friendship was to be a mark of discipleship. In John 11:11 we read: *"...After that he saith unto them, Our friend Lazarus sleepeth; but I go, that I may awake him out of sleep."* Notice that Christ identifies Himself with His disciples as being a friend of Lazarus – *"**Our** friend Lazarus..."*

Of course, Jesus is the Friend that sticks closer than a brother (Proverbs 18:24). In Luke 12:4 we find Him giving advice as a friend: *"And I say unto you my friends, Be not afraid of them that kill the body, and after that have no more that they can do."* It is also as a faithful Friend that He wounds in order to restore or teach those He loves: *"Faithful [are] the wounds of a friend; but the kisses of an enemy [are] deceitful. ... Ointment and perfume rejoice the heart: so [doth] the sweetness of a man's friend by hearty counsel"* (Proverbs 27:6, 9). Peter was rebuked with a look after denying His Lord and Thomas was challenged by His words after doubting His resurrection.

In the Old Testament times, we find that Abraham and Moses were called friends of God: *"And the scripture was fulfilled which saith, Abraham believed God, and it was imputed unto him for righteousness: and he was called the*

Friend of God" (James 2:23). *"And the* LORD *spake unto Moses face to face, as a man speaketh unto his friend"* (Exodus 33:11).

In New Testament times, we find it written of John the Baptist: *"He that hath the bride is the bridegroom: but the friend of the bridegroom, which standeth and heareth him, rejoiceth greatly because of the bridegroom's voice: this my joy therefore is fulfilled"* (John 3:29). When the marriage of the Lamb is come in heaven, John the Baptist will be there. When the King appears to Zion to take her to Himself, John the Baptist will be there also. Why? Because he is the friend of the Bridegroom. In that day and this, those who love pureness of heart shall be friends of the King. *"He that loveth pureness of heart, [for] the grace of his lips the king [shall be] his friend"* (Proverbs 22:11).

Bibliography

Crawford, N. *What the Bible Teaches: Luke* Kilmarnock: John Ritchie, 1989

Gill, J. *An exposition of the Book of Solomon's Song* Paris, Arkansas: The Baptist Standard Bearer, 2002

Hadley, E. C. *The Song of Solomon* Sunbury, Pennsylvania: Believers Bookshelf, reprinted 2006

Nee, Watchman *The Song of Songs* Fort Washington, Pennsylvania: CLC Publications, 2006

Pollock, A. J. *The Amazing Jew* London: The Central Bible Truth Depôt, 1943

Pollock, A. J. *Things Which Must Shortly Come to Pass* London: The Central Bible Truth Depôt, 1948

Slemming, C. W. *These are the Garments* Fort Washington, Pennsylvania: CLC Publications, 2007

Tristram, H.B. *The Natural History of the Bible* Piscataway, New Jersey: Gorgias Press, 2002

Young, R. *Young's Analytical Concordance to the Bible* Peabody, Massachusetts: Hendrickson Publishers, 2002

Index

About the Author

George Stevens was born in Bath, Somerset, England just after World War II. He attended Sunday School and Young Sowers League at Manvers St. Baptist Church as a junior. It was while learning a poem for a prizegiving that he first realised the reality of Christ and that He had risen from the dead. He attended St. Stephen's Church on Lansdown Rd. during his teenage years. He was a member of the choir, (although he would never admit to being a tuneful singer). At the age of about fourteen, he confessed Christ as the Son of God, but had no firm assurance of salvation until he heard the Gospel preached in a small "Brethren" hall in Hounslow. He was in his twenties at the time. He has continued meeting with what would be called historically, the Kelly/Glanton assemblies, although the only label he would boast in is "Christian". Once assured of salvation, one of George's main Bible studies was "Christ in All the Scriptures". This led to a delight in the Song of Solomon to which he has returned many times during his Christian life. This book is one of the results. George was a primary school teacher for about thirty-two years before stepping down from a headship a few years ago.

OTHER BOOKS FROM SCRIPTURE TRUTH PUBLICATIONS

UNDERSTANDING THE OLD TESTAMENT SERIES:

THE TABERNACLE'S TYPICAL TEACHING BY
ALGERNON J POLLOCK

> *ISBN 978-0-901860-65-1 (paperback)*
>
> *236 pages; July 2009*

HOW TO OVERCOME BY JOHN T MAWSON

> *ISBN 978-0-901860-62-0 (paperback)*
>
> *144 pages; April 2009*

DELIVERING GRACE BY JOHN T MAWSON

> *ISBN 978-0-901860-64-4 (paperback)*
>
> *ISBN 978-0-901860-78-1 (hardback)*
>
> *192 pages; March 2007*

ELIJAH: A PROPHET OF THE LORD BY HAMILTON SMITH

> *ISBN 978-0-901860-68-2; (paperback)*
>
> *80 pages; March 2007*

ELISHA: THE MAN OF GOD BY HAMILTON SMITH

> *ISBN 978-0-901860-79-8; (paperback)*
>
> *92 pages; March 2007*

THE GOSPEL IN JOB BY YANNICK FORD

> *ISBN 978-0-901860-76-7 (paperback)*
>
> *ISBN 978-0-901860-77-4 (hardback)*
>
> *112 pages; March 2007*

LESSONS FROM EZRA BY TED MURRAY

> *ISBN 978-0-901860-75-0 (paperback)*
>
> *84 pages; March 2007*

LESSONS FROM NEHEMIAH BY TED MURRAY
ISBN 978-0-901860-86-6 (paperback)
124 pages; August 2008

UNDERSTANDING CHRISTIANITY SERIES:

SEEK YE FIRST BY JOHN S BLACKBURN
ISBN 978-0-901860-61-3 (paperback)
ISBN 978-0-901860-02-6 (hardback)
136 pages; February 2007

GOD AND RELATIONSHIPS BY COR BRUINS
ISBN 978-0-901860-36-1 (paperback)
108 pages; August 2006

"THE EPISTLE OF CHRIST" EDITED BY F. B. HOLE
ISBN 978-0-901860-73-6 (paperback)
140 pages; March 2008

SHORT PAPERS ON THE CHURCH BY HAMILTON SMITH
ISBN 978-0-901860-80-4; (paperback)
96 pages; March 2008

GOD'S INSPIRATION OF THE SCRIPTURES BY WILLIAM KELLY
ISBN 978-0-901860-51-4 (paperback)
ISBN 978-0-901860-56-9 (hardback)
484 pages; March 2007

LECTURES ON THE CHURCH OF GOD BY WILLIAM KELLY
ISBN 978-0-901860-50-7 (paperback)
244 pages; February 2007

ISBN 978-0-901860-55-2 (hardback)
244 pages; March 2007